MEDIOCRITY
IS NOT AN OPTION

Targeting professional success

ROBERT M. CHIUSANO

ISBN: 149956886X
ISBN 13: 9781499568868
Library of Congress Control Number: 2014909310
CreateSpace Independent Publishing Platform
North Charleston, South Carolina

TESTIMONIALS

"Bob is an Aerospace Industry leader who has a remarkable ability to achieve what he commits to. He stands tall amongst his industry peers by expecting no less from others than he asks of himself. Bob worked tirelessly to never disappoint, while doing it the right way, always. He has focused on constantly setting an example for the many team members he mentored throughout his career. We all can learn from the discipline, approaches, and experiences of such a respected and accomplished leader. You will not be disappointed!!"

Preston A. Henne, Fellow AIAA, Fellow RAeS, Member National Academy of Engineering Sr. VP Programs, Engineering & Test, Gulfstream Aerospace Corp. (retired)

"As the Vice President of Business Development at Mead Johnson Nutrition, I rely extensively on my ability to lead cross-functional teams and to develop relationships with companies and individuals throughout the world. I was fortunate enough early in my career to work for Bob and to grasp from him the importance of developing these skill sets via a career plan. The opportunity to read about Bob's life experiences and gain his insight in *"Mediocrity Is Not an Option"* on what it takes to be successful is a priceless read and one I will be recommending to my staff."

Lee Wise, Vice President, Business Development, Mead Johnson Nutrition

"Mediocrity Is Not an Option" provides a unique and practical framework for personal and professional development. Written with energetic prose and practical, real-world examples, this book is unique in emphasizing the importance of being a mentee as a key element of professional development. It is a clarion-call for action that will appeal to a wide audience, from students to new hires to C-Suite executives."

Kevin Michaels, Vice President, ICF International

"He's experienced, engaging, dynamic and passionate. Our college feels so fortunate that our students can learn from, reflect on and be inspired by all of his wisdom and experience. Students quickly relate to Bob's down-to-earth, approachable demeanor. His self-awareness and career development messages in *"Mediocrity Is Not an Option"* resonates well with everyone he meets. This is a must read for anyone looking to jumpstart or re-energize their career."

Ms. Kelli Delfosse, Director of Engineering Professional Development
College of Engineering, University of Iowa

"Mediocrity Is Not an Option" is a MUST read for any aspiring professional. I have known and worked with Bob for over 35 years and personally witnessed many examples of him and his teams achieving great results. The foundation for his exceptional business leadership acumen includes a passion to coach and mentor many others to excel in their careers and become all they can be."

Charles Weber, CFP, Managing Director,
True North Wealth Management

"In his seminars I have seen Bob capture the attention of college undergraduates and inspire them to learn the skills that allow them to take control of their own career destiny. He has the wisdom born of experience and a passionate communication style which creates a vibrant and engaging discussion that draws people in. This book allows students from across the country and across the world to learn about Bob's compelling approach to professional development, and the ideas they learn will serve them well throughout their lives."

Dr. Alec Scranton, Dean of Engineering, University of Iowa

"I personally benefitted from Bob's mentorship so you need to believe what he says in *"Mediocrity Is Not an Option"*. As a mentee, he furthered my development in business acumen, leadership, cross-functional skill development, corporate culture and emotional intelligence. I have learned that mentoring is a contemporary leadership tool to stay in touch with all levels of employees while building bench strength and giving back to your company and is a powerful bridge to personal growth for both the mentee and the mentor. The process provides personal rewards such as broadening your leadership insights, building your personal networks and enriching your diversity and multi-generational perspectives. I now appreciate the importance of mentoring as an on- the -job leadership development tool."

Kevin L. Weiss, Corporate Vice President Human Resources,
L-3 Corporation

DEDICATION

To the members of my family, who put me first and have always been there for me in spite of dealing with their own lives' challenges, thank you. To my mom, who raised five children singlehandedly and dedicated her entire life to her family and her home, I miss you. To my true friends, who put up with all my shortcomings yet still consider me their friend unconditionally while giving more than they take, you are all very special to me. To all those unselfish people around the world who took time away from what was important to them to help me become a more complete person, your commitment to me is truly appreciated and unparalleled.

To Gerry, my very first true mentor, who unselfishly gave his all to me so I would start down the path to becoming all I could be, I truly hope you are proud of me.

To Sal—I wish I had met you so much earlier in my life. I learned from you what living life to the fullest really means. You had such a tremendous impact and influence on what I have become. No man do I admire more. I miss you, Sal. More than you will ever know.

To everyone who took the time to read and constructively critique the manuscript, this one's for you!

Specifically for their work on the cover design, I thank Christopher Chiusano from Boston, Massachusetts and Tim Proctor, Owner of Warrior Digital Marketing Group, Cedar Rapids, Iowa.

And lastly, thanks to Doc for word processing the manuscript and dealing with my reluctance to use available technology that would have made the task easier. Her patience was incredible.

CONTENTS

INTRODUCTION

Perhaps you are wondering who I am. That's totally fair. I've never relished being in the spotlight or highlighted in the media, so it's understandable for you to wonder who I am, what I'm all about, and what you could possibly learn from me.

In saying that, however, I truly want to earn your attention because I have a lot I want to say to you. I want to share my thoughts with you because I believe if you take all I have to say to heart, you will have so many more things to take into account as you think about your life and professional journey. All I ask of you is to give me a chance to make a positive difference in your life starting today. As you soon will see, it all starts with you!

The best way to encourage you to read on is to start with a story—one that is, in a way, a reflection of so many of the things I believe in and that define who I am. In the fall of 2001, I had a mountain adventure planned in Utah, and I was going to drive there from Iowa. I packed the truck and commenced my direct, nonstop journey. When I arrived I was a bit tired from more than twenty hours behind the wheel with little rest along the way. I was focused, excited, and determined to get on with my adventure.

I arrived in Utah in the late evening, got to camp, unpacked, and lay in my tent. I was filled with mixed emotions about work, home, and the adventure. I did not sleep much at all that night as I anticipated what lied ahead for me that next day. The morning came quickly, and my guide came to get me before sunrise to get ready, grab something to eat, and get to the mountain. As we rode our horses from our campsite, located on a mountain-top in the Wasatch Range, to where we would make our descent into the deep valley, my mind was racing with anticipation. The sounds of bugling elk fueled my excitement. I could hear antlers crashing as the bulls fought to establish dominance. I felt so close to a reality that I had only read about or saw on television up to that point.

We tied up our horses, and my long-awaited adventure was finally underway. As we were descending the mountain, I lost my balance while stepping on a slippery and unstable rock I had not seen in the dark; I felt my ankle give way and heard it literally explode. I fell to the ground and looked down at my foot. I could see the entire underside of it from my sitting position. There was no way I was walking back up that mountain.

My guide was a tremendously skilled outdoorsman. He knew a lot about the animals and the local geography. However, at that moment I learned he had never experienced a medical emergency of that magnitude. We could not call for help, as there was no cell reception in the valley, and we were fifty miles away from even a small town. We were alone, just the two of us, and we had a problem of major proportion. We both knew the situation was critical, and we needed to respond accordingly.

Thinking quickly, I asked him to find me some short, stiff branches, and with those and my shirt I made a splint to stabilize my leg and foot. I gave him my equipment and asked him to hike back up the mountain and meet me on top. I also asked if when he got to the top, he could get to a place where he could call the University Sports Clinic in Salt Lake City, notify them of my injury, and get instructions on what to do once we got off that mountain. He responded affirmatively and left to get on with the tasks at hand.

I had to get myself up that mountain. There was no other choice. Once on top, I needed to get on the horse and ride back to camp and on to the clinic. I fought off the shock into which I could feel my body and mind slipping. I had to get out of there.

So I focused, put everything else out of my mind, and made a plan. I was in great physical condition (other than my ankle), and there was no one on Earth more determined than I was at that moment. I got up the mountain by sliding on my backside, pushing myself up the steep terrain with my good leg, and dragging the broken one. Along the way I used my arms to support myself and push my way up, making a few feet of progress with each action. It took me four and a half hours going nonstop to get to the top. I never once thought about failure. I never thought about the severity of my injury or the pain. I never worried or panicked but just remained focused on the need to get out of there. Interestingly enough, no other viable option entered my mind. This was on me.

My guide was waiting for me as we had planned. He had gotten the horses ready. He had also found a place with adequate cell service and made a call to the sports clinic, so they knew our situation and were expecting us. My injury was very severe; it required a total of six operations to put my ankle back together so that my quality of life and functionality could be improved to acceptable levels. It took me about eighteen months of procedures, therapy, setbacks and a tremendous amount of drive and determination not to let that mountain ever beat me. That was NEVER an option for me, ever.

Challenges motivate me, and to deal with them head on gives tremendous utility to my life. I love true challenges, and

I take them personally. The stress, energy, and passion that come from taking on things others might prefer not to deal with are tremendously exciting for me. I am totally convinced that how we react to any challenges we face in our lives offers an entire set of lessons in itself. Assessing a situation, developing a plan to deal with it, and executing the plan are lessons that translate to all aspects of our lives.

To an even greater extent, having the ability to recognize our shortcomings or not having the necessary tools to deal with what life throws at us can be rewarding. The questions we all have to ask ourselves are: Will we ever be willing to understand these things? Can we accept them as opportunities for bettering ourselves, let alone have the will and desire to do what it takes to become all we are capable of becoming? I will help you think through all this as you make a personal commitment to take responsibility for your personal and professional development.

The experience on the mountain taught me a lot about myself. The lessons and skills I applied that day all continue to serve me well today. I had a problem, I was totally responsible for what happened, and I was responsible for dealing with it. I made a plan and mustered the focus, energy, and passion to execute it successfully, and in the end it all worked out. What I realized is that life's experiences are no different whether they're personal or professional in nature. You must hold yourself accountable and deal with the outcomes of your decisions. No excuses. No blame. Accept, plan, and act!

Throughout this book I will expose you to many things, and you will learn a lot more about my transformation from troubled teen to chief operating officer of a Fortune 500 multibillion-dollar business. I will share stories about some of the people, experiences, and lessons I know were instrumental in helping me determine what I wanted to accomplish. It is vital that you truly believe that everything I say in this book applies to you and that you can utilize it to help you find your personal and professional platforms regardless of whether you have individual aspirations or care to play a role in a larger organization. It doesn't matter—student, individual contributor, entrepreneur, business owner, or executive, it's all the same and has direct application to each and every one of us, including you! This concept applies regardless of your age, gender, cultural background, and the like. Each and every one of these variables will likely impact *how* you think about your current situation and *what*, if anything, you're going to do about it.

I came from the Northeast, a town called Schenectady in upstate New York. Even though my dad was a successful business executive, a messy divorce left my mom and our family with the need to live well within our means. We had a modest household. My schooling took a backseat, and I treated everything social as a priority. I was headed for trouble. I channeled my endless energy toward mostly the wrong places, and I lived for each day. Woodstock was a little over an hour away from where I lived, so of course I made participating in the original music festival in 1969 a mission of top priority. Drinking, partying, and at times hanging out with the wrong crowd, and brushes with the law were commonplace. That's not all that bad and not so uncommon for someone in his early teens. However, I was lashing out to an extreme with no end in sight!

I was the oldest boy in a broken home, and my mom and my siblings relied heavily on me for emotional and financial support. That amount of responsibility at twenty years old will get one's attention quickly. Then I was drafted and served our country proudly for six years. During that time I at least marginally addressed the importance of thinking about my life and how

I wanted to spend it. I had matured, but not to anywhere near the level at which I could say I had any direction in life.

After my honorable discharge, I was living the dream, or so I thought. I was residing at home, owned a sports car, and came and went as I pleased. I was making a great wage for that time, and my mom and siblings were taken care of, but I was still living for each day. Not one time did I think about tomorrow, let alone short-term or long-term prospects for my life. *Today* was what I lived for; one day at a time. So what did I have to worry about?

In reality, even though I didn't realize it, there was a lot that should have concerned me. At the time I didn't understand that what I really needed was for someone to kick me in the backside and help me get my head screwed on straight. I required something to get me to think more about how I wanted to spend my life because on my own it wasn't going to happen.

In the next ten chapters, I'm going to do my very best to share many aspects of my personal and professional transformations. I'm driven to share my thoughts with you so that you can take what I have experienced and apply it to your specific situation. I want you to put yourself in the best possible position to reach your full potential. It is important that you truly understand and accept the lead role *you* play in creating your legacy. Last but not least, what I really want is help you get to a point where you will feel as passionate about my beliefs as I do. It is not important what your personal or career aspirations are or how aggressive or lofty they may be. I want you to be convinced that they will apply in some way to each and every one of us without exception.

As with just about anything I have attempted to accomplish in my adult life, I wanted to be a part of something special and someday be in a position to share my experiences with others. The time is now for me to do that. The concepts I'll introduce are those I am most passionate about, and I am confident that once I have shared them, and others understand and practice them, I will be in a position to make real differences in people's lives. This, I believe, is my primary calling in life. I do my best every day never to forget that and to live my life to its fullest.

I did not know I wanted to be an engineer until I was twenty-four years old; even after I started my formal engineering education, I still was not sure. The answer changed almost immediately upon my entering the job force soon after graduating from engineering school. While I deeply respected and enjoyed the academic rigor and challenge of the engineering field, it was simply a job to me, not a passion. If I were not excited to go to work each day, how could I learn, have fun, and make a difference? That was the point in my life at which I recognized that satisfying these three criteria formed the basis for how much passion I could put into every effort. You will see me refer to these criteria numerous times throughout this book. They gave me a sense of purpose, direction, and focus in everything I set out to accomplish. The same thing can happen to you. Perhaps it already has, or the turmoil associated with not having this sense of accomplishment or satisfaction is ongoing inside you currently.

My professional endgame changed in a big way and changed multiple times throughout my life. Initially I did not want to continue my career in the field of engineering. I came to realize I wanted to be more involved in the business aspects of the company and spend less time focusing on product development. After a few short years of serving as a program manager, the concept of leading people became a passion of mine, so I began to focus my skill development efforts in that area. This process worked for me multiple times throughout my career. I actually changed roles thirteen different times during my corporate tenure. The desire and passion to become all I could be was the driving force and instigated each and every move.

If you follow my guidance, take responsibility for your development, and act accordingly, odds are your answer will evolve as well! The world is filled with aspiring individuals, from those who don't have clues what they want to do to those whose directions are quite clear.

As I began my engineering career in a corporate environment, I was concerned that a longer-term perspective on my professional development did not exist. My direct supervisors at the time did not identify career planning as important, nor did I spend a lot of time thinking about it. That was a *huge* issue. I realized this during my first series of annual performance reviews. I sat down with my supervisor to talk about how I was doing at my job, and all we did was assess to what extent I had achieved the goals we had established a year earlier. We spent virtually no time discussing critical things such as my skills, my strengths, and areas requiring further development. There was no dialogue about what challenges might be next for me. I felt that a number of contributing factors were at play: issues such as management's discomfort with having the tough yet crucial conversation about where and how I could improve my skill sets.

I can't and won't blame it solely on my supervisors because my attitude was also clearly an issue. Specifically, I am referring to my inability to accept criticism whether it was constructive or not. I didn't want to hear it! Does this sound familiar? If we are truly honest with ourselves, we will recognize the feedback we receive has merit and applies to us. It is highly likely the feedback will not be a surprise, and it is equally likely that knowing someone noticed and identified our shortcomings will create anxiety. Later in the book, I will encourage you to embrace the feedback and provide some insight on what to do about it!

Remember: like it or not, almost everything in life is some form of competition. Do you have the desire to be different, stand above the rest, and be the one others look to when it's time to accomplish great things? If you do, then you have to be ready to do what it takes to make that happen. It's not just going to occur. That's what I'm going to ask you to think a lot about as I help you with understanding the process and the tools to make this all become a reality. I do not want mediocrity to be an option you choose because that puts your life's fulfillment at risk.

In chapter one I'll ask you to look in the mirror and be honest about what you see in yourself. I'll encourage you to face your fears and obstacles aggressively, and, at the same time, capitalize on your strengths. You will learn to appreciate that not everyone sees in you what you see when you look in the mirror. I'll also ask you to seek input from those who are different from you in thought, background, values, beliefs, and experiences. I will encourage you to *listen to*—not just hear—the diverse perspectives of others and welcome the dialogues openly. Be gracious in seeking and receiving insight, knowing that humility and approachability are basic to learning what you need to know. It will also become apparent that you should reflect on this feedback and once again accept the responsibility to do something with what you learn!

It's never too early or too late to think about what you want your professional legacy to be. A simple way to get started is to spend some time thinking about it as if you were creating your own personal brand. How do you want to define yourself? What sets you apart from the rest? What makes you special? These are all very pertinent questions, and the answers play a crucial part in creating your career development plan. The subject matter of this book, while perhaps having more impact for high school and college students or those in the early stages of their professional careers, applies to anyone who wants to personally affect his or her professional destiny. Wherever this places you, I would like you to imagine your last day of work, thinking about what you have achieved during your professional career. I want this to be an incredibly rewarding moment for you in your life, knowing you did all you set out to do and more. Along the way, you must accept the fact that your perspectives will change over time, and constantly remind yourself that this is not an exact science. It's called living a progressive career development lifestyle, and becomes an art form over time.

You will learn to recognize the critical roles people play in all aspects of your life. It starts with your taking ownership of yourself. If you don't absorb any other of my guiding principles, remember this throughout the book: *you* own the responsibility to take charge of your life. Don't waste time or energy looking around for someone to blame for your lack of development. This is not to say that several others in your circle of influence do not play important roles in this. In fact, you will soon learn the network you're developing is quite important. However, *you* determine your development in the end. I have mentored thousands of employees, students, friends, and professional associates throughout my life. I can say without reservation that at least initially, the majority fell short in the area of understanding and accepting personal ownership. This is not an incremental piece of advice; accepting personal ownership is instrumental. Start thinking about this and personalizing it right now—*no excuses*! *You* have the ability to control your destiny.

Then I will continually coach you to add the practice of lifelong learning to your renewed emphasis on personal accountability. You will better understand how important learning something new every day is to the energy you bring to all aspects of your life. I'll introduce you to the notion of how important it is to have fun in all you do, and how effective the energy that results from enjoying the role you play can be in motivating yourself and those around you! Remember that the opposite is also true: lethargy and mediocrity are contagious behaviors. I want you to experience the tremendous gratification that results from having truly made a difference regardless of how it manifests. Making a difference has served as a major motivator in encouraging me to seek, take on, and conquer every challenge I face. True leaders pursue those who want to play a role in making great things happen, and you'll know when you're making progress; opportunities will seek you out in both the personal and professional aspects of your life. You can bet on it!

So now, as you start getting your head wrapped around accepting responsibility for your development, I want you to keep these additional thoughts constantly close at hand:

- ➲ Do you respect and value yourself without bias?

- ➲ Is working and living in an environment where people are treated as difference makers rather than necessary commodities important to you?

- ➲ Is the person or organization you work for or plan to work for as interested or more interested in helping facilitate your reaching your full potential as they are in focusing on their own success?

- ➲ Do you accept ownership for your actions and the outcomes of your decisions?

Thinking about these points has aided me as I've faced making assignment or career change decisions. These pieces of advice had a tremendous influence on how I weighed the career opportunities that came my way. The development, progression, and mobility of many of those I have mentored are a direct testimonial to the impact of these considerations.

I will ask you to take inventory of yourself and your skills. As you do, take special notice of your shortcomings and compare those to the skills you have identified as necessary for you to master in order to move ahead, and to get one step closer to your next objective.

I will ask you to learn the importance of embracing the contributions of mentors and any others you see as influential in your life. As time passes, hopefully you will embrace how you must commit to paying it forward, with you serving as a mentor to other aspiring individuals and making real differences in their lives! Remember: no road leads directly to your promised land. Setbacks, roadblocks, politics, and the unforeseen can all come into play. Have the staying power; remain committed to yourself and to your development. Adding to your skill set takes time, energy, research, and patience, and the skill set is never complete. You must constantly embrace the concept of practicing lifelong learning. You're never going to be done developing. Stay the course. Do not yield to the impediments—and there will be many.

Comfort zone is a term you need to delete from your vocabulary starting today. In many ways, a comfort zone implies complacency, mediocrity, and stagnation. And mediocrity is not an option. If you can learn to understand mediocrity and how limiting it can be to you and those around you, much of what I have to share with you will take on a whole new level of meaning, and its impact will be more significant.

I was at my new dentist's office one day. I was having trouble with a tooth, a residual effect from previous dental treatment received elsewhere. I had been looking for a new dental professional who was far more current on technique and technology, and through recommendations from my family I found her. It didn't take me long to appreciate her talent and skills, and to develop an extreme level of confidence in her abilities.

After a very thorough exam, she informed me she was totally convinced that I needed a root canal, and she would refer me to an endodontist (a root canal specialist) for further treatment. I am not sure why, but something made me ask her, "Don't you do root canals?" She reluctantly said she had done a few in dental school and some in private practice, but she felt it was best she refer me to someone who did them all the time. She was doing what she felt was right to ensure I received the very best treatment.

While I did my best to understand her perspective, this did not sit well with me at the time. I knew she had the capability, and I was highly confident in her skills. I felt extremely comfortable with her expertise and wanted to encourage her strongly to be more confident in herself. I did not see this as a medical risk at all but as an opportunity to receive professional treatment and make a difference in someone's life. There was no way in hell I was leaving that office to see another dentist when the person who could do it was standing there right in front of my eyes. She, perhaps, lacked the confidence in taking it on for whatever reason. She felt uncomfortable doing something complex that was out of her comfort zone, yet she had the skill set to do the job correctly. I took the opportunity to push her out of that mind-set and told her quite directly she was doing my root canal, and that she did not really have an option because I was not leaving that chair. Certainly, had the medical risk been significant, we would not have proceeded, I trusted her. This had absolutely nothing to do with dentistry for me; she had that domain mastered. It had everything to do with encouraging her to take a chance, to take a prudent risk by accomplishing something she was most capable of doing but did not yet have the confidence to do routinely.

I truly believe that in that one afternoon, her professional legacy began to change for the good. Since that time, she has successfully performed hundreds of root canals of varying degrees of complexity. She has grown both her skills and her confidence and expanded the brand image of her practice at the same time. I despise the term *comfort zone*, and I would not accept her reasoning. As successful and talented as she was, even she needed some encouragement and for someone to believe in her; the rest was up to her. Many of us are no different.

You will learn more about this as you read on. It applies to us all! Before you can expect others to move out of their comfort zones, you need to practice it yourself. I will help you with this challenge later in the book.

You will also see it's not all about you. So as you learn, develop, and contribute at greater levels, I will encourage you to step up and accept the responsibility to assist others as they work to define their professional legacies. Be the type of coach or mentor you would expect others to be for you!

I will expose you to my firm belief that if you truly want to lead and not simply manage, you must possess certain skill sets that pertain directly to you relating to people in a far more effective way. These "soft" skills are very instrumental in developing your personal and professional influences on others and will clearly improve the quality of your relationships and experiences over time.

As you develop and become more visible as a leader, you will need to become far more cognizant of the shadow your leadership casts on others. How you appear becomes who you are. Take notice of your body language. Again, this applies in all aspects of your life. You are not only what you think you are; you also become a force for others based on how they see you.

One of the most common and consistent questions I get from many people is, does aspiring to become all you can be have a direct impact on one's work and life balance? I will expound upon this later, but I will tell you right up front that the answer is yes! I will share with you how you can go about trying to achieve a better personal and professional balance in your life, but I will also tell you that in almost all cases, with additional success and responsibility come sacrifices that will have some impact on your personal life. It's important that you be aware of that going in; if anyone tells you otherwise, challenge it vigorously because it's simply not true. This is not to say you can't work to achieve improvements in this balance; in fact, you owe it to both yourself and those around you to do just that. However, doing this will require compromise and persistence over the long-term.

I ask you to keep an open mind about everything you currently believe to be truths in reference to your personal and professional development. Be totally open to listen and consider a different way; perhaps a more creative and effective way to accomplish your objectives. Pay attention, and embrace the concepts I will lay out for you by putting them into practice starting today and continuing every day from now on without exception. I want to encourage you always to challenge your existing beliefs and paradigms. What is your calling in life? What is your life's purpose? Each and every one of us has a focus, a specific reason for being here. I also believe achieving that purpose is not a given, nor is it guaranteed. You will know it when it happens.

The first step in making this a reality comes from within by understanding who we are and what we need to do to achieve our purpose and our full potential. Once you have committed to taking charge, your path will become more tangible and your destination more clear. It is never too early or too late to start. The time is now! And, last but not least, take this advice and put it in the bank: *mediocrity is not an option!*

I hope you enjoy this book, and I wish you nothing but the best of luck, happiness, and prosperity—however you define them.

CHAPTER 1

LOOK IN THE MIRROR

I was ten years old, and it was springtime. I should have been outside playing, but instead I was sitting on the floor in front of the TV. The president of the United States was giving a speech to the entire nation on making it to the moon before the end of the decade. I was quite young, but he still made quite an impression on me. At that time I could not fathom how we could land a man on the moon in nine years or fewer; it was way above my head. I remember equating it to walking on water. Also, traits such as stage presence, conviction, vision, energy, and the ability to look to the future and set a course for tomorrow were all unfamiliar concepts to me at that young age. Yet for some reason, I simply admired these and other behaviors in the president and thought I wanted them for myself. He made such an impression on me. Even at that age the seeds were planted, and, while they weren't fully understood and didn't germinate for quite some time, I recall that experience as one step of many that helped change my life years later.

On July 20, 1969, *Apollo 11* landed the first human beings on the moon, beating the timeline established eight years earlier. What lessons we can learn from that experience alone! How do we get to the point at which we know who we are, what we are made of, and what we need to do? How do we learn to grow and develop into people who are much more robust, exciting, and interesting, with the ability to accomplish great things? If you don't remember anything else throughout the course of reading this book, remember that you own the responsibility for your development. While others will affect your journey, you have to look no farther than yourself for the person who is accountable. It's time you take a long, hard look in the mirror before we can go one step farther.

Throughout my life I have encountered a tremendous number of individuals who quickly lashed out at, blamed, or offloaded responsibility onto others. There are many reasons for this: it is easier to preserve your image to yourself or perhaps to fool others; it is even more natural to push the cause onto others.

Look no farther than yourself.

While it may in the short-term provide you some comfort to think you are not to blame, behaving in this fashion almost guarantees your developmental demise.

I found from my own challenges in accepting personal accountability that blaming others was, in some odd way, in part a reflection of behaviors I saw in myself. For example, lashing out at others about someone else was a frequent occurrence earlier in my career. I remember interviewing for a job at the start of my career. I'm sure I applied only because it offered both a salary increase and a reporting-level increase. But it was clearly a job I did not truly want nor one for which I was qualified. While I will talk far more about this soon enough, suffice it to say here that the skills necessary for me to do the job properly were of little to no interest to me.

Still, when I received the news that I wasn't chosen, it angered me. I even contemplated leaving the company! How could I not have gotten an offer? Then I began to bad-mouth the hiring manager, the process, the human resources department, and whoever else was standing next to me. The reality was that I'd had no business applying for that job in the first place, and I had done so for all the wrong reasons; it was all on me. You see, I may have been driven, but I was *not* committed to my development. My complaining about my supervisors not being able to have a meaningful discussion with me about my career was, in a way, a reflection of my inability to act in a similar fashion with the people on my team.

It is not clear when or how I came to this realization or if it happened quickly or evolved over time. I like to think it was the result of feedback I received from others. Perhaps it was a culmination of similar observations and experiences I gained along the way that helped me recognize that it all needed to start with me. It became very clear to me that in order for me to have any chance to do something about how others behaved, I needed first to deal with the sources of my behavior by looking at myself. Please, don't misunderstand me: there is a positive side to this. Not all the behaviors I placed on the shoulders of others were detrimental in nature, and I made it a point to assume innocence and look for the good in others first. Over time, when I observed and commented on the positive attributes I saw in others—energy, passion, forgiveness, generosity, and humility—I realized, perhaps indirectly, these were reflections of myself. I believe this was how it became essential for me to recognize the importance of better understanding myself— who I am and what I can become. This is, quite simply, called self-awareness.

So, what can I tell you now that will help you better understand who you are? First, before I ask you to look in the mirror and tell me what you really see, I need to explain this concept of self-awareness more and what you can do to improve your capability. It is also very important for you to master this concept in advance of my asking you to form relationships with mentors and to focus more on building an extensive network and expanding your circle of influence.

> *To achieve, you must be both driven and committed.*

If you are very self-aware, the next several pages will, at a minimum, serve as a reminder of how to keep your skills sharp, and you may even learn something new that will take these skills to a higher level. However, if you're more like the majority of individuals I've had the honor of mentoring or coaching over the years, I am confident you will soon gain some insights on how to become far better at improving the level of your self-awareness.

Now, what can I suggest you focus on to improve the quality of your self-awareness? First, do all you can to force yourself out of your comfort zone. I have briefly mentioned the concept of the comfort zone and how breaking out of it can have a significant impact on your life. Try as best you can to put yourself in a position to experience new things in spite of our natural tendency as humans to play it safe.

I recall one of the first times I was forced out of my comfort zone. It happened on my first day of basic training after entering the air force. There were drill instructors barking commands at me from all directions. That alone was enough to get my attention, but in many cases, and quite intentionally, the commands were conflicting, designed in such a way that no matter which command I followed, I was not following others' orders. That created even more chaos and anxiety. I so desperately wanted to speak up, defend my actions, and stand up for myself, but that was not going to happen. Speaking back to persons of higher authority without permission would have put me in further disfavor.

So there I was, perhaps for the very first time in my life, being told what to do and how to do it with no ability to offer my perspectives or views. I didn't get a vote. It was clearly way beyond my personal comfort zone, and it was by design. It was all about breaking me down in order to build me back up. From that experience I began to learn how to listen, understand the chain of command, respect authority, and do as I was told unconditionally. All of that and more was possible because I stepped, or in this case, was pushed way out of my comfort zone.

First, when we are put or place ourselves in situations that are less than familiar, we are faced with the challenge of developing our responses to each of them. You must look at them not just as risks but also as opportunities to learn something more about yourself, add a new set of experiences to your life story, and set the stage for being better prepared the next time similar circumstances present themselves. I am also going to ask you to try hard to seek these opportunities out actively versus simply waiting for them to occur. I can guarantee that if you do as I suggest, you will learn things about yourself that you were not aware of, and at the same time you will be energized and develop improved self-confidence. How good is that?

Second, I suggest you try even harder to self-reflect when listening to the experiences of others. There is a *huge* difference between simply lending an ear to someone who is sharing an experience with you and being truly engaged in the conversation and listening to what is being shared. Through listening you can reflect on how others' experiences relate to situations in your life and how you might best deal with similar situations should they arise. If we don't become more proficient in our listening skills, we will not be able to comprehend, evaluate, and apply what others have told us. Use every conversation as an opportunity to learn more about yourself and as a means to grow.

Third, to help you focus on improving your self-awareness, take some time on occasion to write down your most memorable experiences. Specifically, document the experiences that were most notable, remarkable, and worthy of your attention. I have found this useful in a few ways: it allows you to capture the moment before it's lost and overcome by other events; it will prepare you for the opportunity to self-reflect, learn, and apply what you've discovered at a later time; and it will most likely come in handy when you are in a position to coach others. Remember, each and every experience is an opportunity to learn, grow, and share your journey with others.

Improving your self-awareness will enhance your ability to have more of an impact on others. It will help you become more adept at identifying your strengths and weaknesses, which in turn will allow you to place additional emphasis on skill development and capitalizing on your areas of strength. Enhanced motivation goes a long way toward providing the energy and staying power you will need to become all you can be. Grasping a better understanding of which behaviors and actions cause less than acceptable performance is an important step in knowing what to address to improve your performance outcomes. You will find yourself energized and motivated to remove the impediments that stand in your way, and to deal with stress and anxiety in a much more effective manner.

I am hopeful that you now better understand and appreciate the importance of looking at yourself in the mirror. The world is full of excuses for why we will not change what we spend time on—statements such as "I'm too busy," "It's not pressing enough right now," "It's too difficult," "I'm this way for a reason," "This will pass over time and it will get better," "No one's ever told me that before," "I don't believe that," "I don't make mistakes," and "It's not my responsibility." The list could go on forever! Do any of these excuses sound familiar? They likely will; I know I used all of these and more at one time or another. Don't waste your time or energy on this. Put your attention toward serving a much better purpose.

As with anything, I needed some form of motivation to change my behavior. I recall there was a time very early in my career when I would practice what I called "management by bat." I thought calling people out in public, almost to the point of humiliation, was an effective way to get things done. I felt it was their fault that they fell short, and I was not in a frame of mind to listen to excuses. Whether it was being late for an appointment, missing a design delivery date, or not getting something we had promised a customer on time, to me there was never a valid explanation. I treated everything as an excuse, and it almost always resulted in my lashing out.

While it may have been effective at that point in time, I had no concept of the collateral longer-term damage I was creating through my actions. Word traveled quickly that I was intimidating, and, instead of commitment and respect, fear and distrust resulted. I didn't know any better and just thought that was the way things got done.

But I did notice one thing that was instrumental in changing my behavior: almost immediately after each incident in which I would blame others for their shortcomings, I would feel terrible. I found myself upset after the fact, knowing my actions had been demeaning and hurtful to others. So, what can we learn from this? After looking in the mirror, examining myself, and recognizing the chaos I was causing, I made it a point to pause before lashing out; then I made attempts to try another way. By explaining my disappointment, restating my expectations, and offering my assistance, I would gain others' attention, and the outcomes would be far more positive. I remember going into a verbal tirade at a factory operator who didn't follow a design change that impacted her assembly procedure. She basically told me to shut up and reminded me I would "catch more bees with honey than with vinegar." Her point was valid, short, and effective. She taught me a lesson that continues to serve me well—most of the time, at least. I needed to get past the excuses and have some reason to change my behavior, and to put my mind and energy into improving myself continuously, each and every day.

Lessons can come at any stage in life; it's what we do with them that is important. As I think back over my life, another one of the most significant and impactful experiences also came at quite an early age. It also came unexpectedly, and its method of delivery was clearly unorthodox. But it was an experience that in its own way changed my life for the better.

I was sixteen and parked in our driveway. My father was in the passenger seat, teaching me how to drive. I was practicing for my driver's license test, but little did I know a much larger lesson was looming. For whatever reason, my father decided to lash out about my poor study habits and my lack of focus on anything other than my social life. He ended our talk by telling me, "Robert, you're not going to make anything of yourself. You are going to waste your life and will die a bum." He used those exact words. I remember everything about that short lesson. I could not accept what he said as defining my life for the long-term. While it truly hurt and was a poorly delivered message, I heard it loud and clear.

Though he may not have realized it then, my father forced me to look inward, to see myself as he saw me and not as I wanted to be seen. It was years before I did anything about it. This lesson again came into life after my time spent serving our country. I had grown up and was ready to take a good look at myself, to see what my father had seen. It was time to prove him wrong and to make myself proud. That day with my father and the time spent serving my country were quite instrumental in putting me on a course to make that a reality.

I suggest you do the same thing with respect to dedicating yourself to your development. You too can use a disappointing event in your life to initiate a change in focus. Don't do what I did at first—I blurred the true meaning of the message because of the tone and manner in which it was delivered. Perhaps it was

It's what we do with all we learn that matters.

age, my lack of maturity, or my state of mind at that time. But I encourage you to listen carefully and search for the real messages, putting aside the emotions. The outcome, as I eventually realized, was what impacted me most. Use experiences like these to create the energy and focus you need to fuel the changes in behavior and focus that will help you move forward in a new and better way.

The next challenge you may likely face is finding the time in what might be an already full schedule to do what it takes. This is where many people give in or lose energy. In order for you to expect anything different, something needs to change. In this case you must make the time. Is this easier said than done? It depends on you! I suggest you start by looking at all the things that currently fill your day and determine the purpose and value of what currently consumes your time. I am confident that you spend some portion of your time on things that provide little to no value, that are trivial or lack importance. You will need to make some trade-offs, again relying on taking ownership.

Start by voiding your day of enough non-value-added activities to make time for something you deem quite important. This will serve as another test of your level of commitment by doing what it takes to make the time. Simple things will help! Change your going to bed or waking up pattern. How about spending less time on your smartphone, checking in on social networks, gaming, texting, posting, or tweeting? I'm not telling you to stop these behaviors; I'm simply telling you that in order to make time to spend on something that can truly change your life, you will need to spend less time on things that do not carry the same degree of importance. Those things can wait a few hours, and the world will not stop!

I am not in a position to tell you exactly what actions will work for you. However, I am in a position to guarantee you that some portion of your time is spent on tasks that provide little to no value and/or should be of less importance to you than your self-development. You need to find out what those things are and make the adjustments in how you prioritize and spend your time. It starts with you!

Once you are able to make the time, the next step is determining where to start. Let's keep it simple: I suggest you start by writing down things you believe you do well. Perhaps define the attributes you know about yourself and ones that others would use to describe you. I also suggest you not list

> *Each of us has only so much time; treat it with the respect it deserves.*

only attributes one may define as "professionally related." Do not limit yourself; *anything goes.* I would challenge you to name an attribute that is solely applicable in either a personal or professional domain. It will be difficult at least. Positive attributes, such as good communication skills, willingness to help others, ability to think quickly on your feet, dependability, and following through on commitments apply in all aspects of your life.

Take your time when developing this list. Do some research; gain the perspectives of others along the way. Where possible make an attempt to provide a couple of real, meaningful examples of how those attributes manifest in your life. For example, let's take the attribute of doing what you say you will do—honoring your commitments. Perhaps you can reflect on a challenging project in which you committed to executing your work within the budgeted time frame and cost, and you were successful. Or recall a time when your ability to communicate effectively was instrumental in you and/or your team overcoming an obstacle while accomplishing something very special.

The keys in this step are to remain open, dig deep, be honest with yourself, and take your time. Clarity and depth are important. You may also find that first focusing on the positive will kick-start the entire self-reflection aspect of planning in a more constructive mind-set. This in turn will generate much-needed energy as you move on to the more challenging task that lies ahead: dealing with your shortcomings.

At the end of this chapter is a template for a skill set checklist that you can use, build on, and tailor to your liking. It will help you better visualize the ideas I am talking about here. There is nothing magical in this template, but it's a great place to start!

Let's move on now to one of the more challenging aspects of this entire process: identifying your shortcomings. Again, anything goes here, but the challenges are more robust. While your first inclination will be either to gloss over this part or even say you have no shortcomings, by doing this you will only be fooling yourself. None of us on Earth is perfect, nor are we as good as we think we are. I recommend you reflect on all that positive energy you created while assessing your strengths and start to apply it here.

The key is to be honest with yourself; no one knows you as well as you do. Now it's time to let go of the natural instinct to bury your shortcomings and begin the process of not only defining what they are but also dealing with them. You can turn them into strengths. This aspect is going to challenge you in many ways as it has many of us. I would like to offer you some insight on how to deal with the many challenging impediments you'll face while inventorying your shortcomings. You can create a similar list as you did for your strengths, or you can put both the strengths and shortcomings on one list and use a strength level rating system to differentiate them from each other. Again, the template offered at the end of this chapter will form the basis for you to document this activity.

Initially, work hard to be as impartial and unbiased as possible. Also, don't worry about being balanced in regard to numbers of strengths and weaknesses. This is meant as an exercise in which you can be honest with yourself, be fair, and remain open-minded. It will be next to impossible to get on a path to self-improvement if you are unable to deal with reality! Sometimes the truth really hurts. You will need to learn how to deal with the realization that none of us is anywhere near perfect. The sooner you learn to accept this, the better.

I have another personal experience to share to help make my point. I love to talk and can tell stories all day long. Even as a younger man, I was confident and used that sure-footedness as a license to talk even more, sometimes nonstop. I think I fell in love with listening to myself. I am sure that was acceptable at times, yet I am sure there were an equal number of times—if not more—when that behavior was destructive. I would cut people off and not pay attention to what they had to say. In a way I was telling them that what they had to say was not important to me.

Once I was on a verbal roll in an MBA study group. I was talking eloquently about a customer relationship management experience as if I were the only one who had ever had one. Finally, two of the three other people politely asked me to be quiet, take a breath, and give someone else a chance to share, reminding me that this was a study group, by the way. Their words literally stopped me in my tracks, and I was taken aback at first. I didn't say another word for the rest of our time that day. I left angry and upset at them. The reality was they were absolutely correct in both the message and the delivery, and I knew it all along. My point is, if it is reality, deal with it! I can't say I mastered the art of listening right away, but the awareness to work on this aspect of my development became very clear that day.

Next, you must avoid a lack of clarity or any degree of ambiguity in understanding your shortcomings as much as possible. More often than not, these challenges to your skills, behaviors, values, or experiences will serve as the most significant impediments to your development. If you can buy-in to that concept, the importance of being clear and thorough will be underscored.

As you attempt to take account of the areas that challenge you most, your natural tendency will be to give these attributes *too much* credit. I am not implying they are not important—I just told you they are. However, they are not life threatening, so please keep them in their proper context. I suggest you view them as challenges, barriers, and obstacles that require your time and attention if you are going to grow beyond your current level of development. Your ability to be honest, unbiased, balanced, and clear in defining these areas for improvement is important. The extent to which you focus on addressing them will determine the degree to which you will be effective in reaching your full potential.

Please ensure that you have fully documented your strengths and areas requiring additional focus. Use the sample template provided at the end of this chapter if you find it useful; either way, it's important that you write them down. Remember, it is equally important to list examples of how each of these specific skills manifests in your life. We want to give meaning and credibility to your assessment by bringing your skills inventory to life. At this point it is not crucial that this list contain assessments of skills you may think are required for a certain role or a series of roles, or even life in general. Remember, this is a living document and will evolve over time as you develop and address your skill set needs. There will be more on this later, but for now, simply do the best possible job in documenting things just as you see them at this time in your life.

Turning shortcomings into strengths is masterful.

I have introduced the concept of documenting your strengths and your areas for improvement as you see them. You might think you're finished with the self-assessment part of the process. However, while you are off to a reasonable start, there is so much more work to be done here. Putting extra time and effort into your preparation will always set you apart from others.

The next task is to list the things you truly enjoy spending time on, and on the same list, those things you simply do not like doing. Anything would apply here, both personally and professionally. Things you enjoy doing won't require much from you to become motivated because you enjoy them. Your tendency will be to migrate to them naturally. The real emphasis here should be on those things you don't like doing. Some examples of characteristics that fell into this category early on for me were public speaking, air travel, direct sales, conflict management, and decision making. All of these things were out of my comfort zone.

The thought of getting up in front of people to speak frightened the hell out of me, so I avoided it at all costs. Air travel was another thing that caused me great turmoil. How could I ever aspire to be a global presence if I was afraid to fly? Then there was the phase of my career when I was troubled with indecision. I was afraid to make a bad decision, so I avoided making any at all. There is not a right or wrong answer here; you are simply trying to make an account of everything you can think of that can impact your development. If you think of it in that way, you will be just fine. Recognizing, understanding, and accepting these issues are necessary first steps.

While the primary purpose of this entire effort is to focus on your development, there will clearly be a relationship between what you like and dislike in both your professional and personal lives and what you tend to focus on in your actions. Don't spend a lot of time worrying about whether an attribute relates more to one aspect of your life or the other. The point is to identify everything on your mind that can either be an impediment to your development or enable it. People naturally tend to shy away from things they dislike. But that approach likely will not serve you well because you always need to do what is required, like it or not! The other benefit of taking this extra step is that it allows you to address each characteristic and make a determination on how you want to deal with it. As a minimum you will have identified them and included them in your plan.

Once you have thought about all the types of characteristics discussed so far, you need to take some time to review them in the aggregate. This will help you fine-tune your thoughts, deal with any overlaps or omissions, and ensure you are completely satisfied with your self-assessment.

Earlier I mentioned how you see yourself, what you see when you look in the mirror, and how those may or may not be the same as how others see you. There are many reasons for this, but the fact remains that it is now time to bring your self-assessment to another level. It's time to work smart and focus your energy by getting the perspectives of others. While doing this you will again need to be honest with yourself. You will need to be flexible and choose individuals carefully and constantly remind yourself that your objective is to become the best you can be.

When selecting the number of individuals to help you, remember it just needs to be manageable. You will be asking them to spend time assessing you, applying the same process you used to assess yourself. The most important factor is the quality of the people you select. Let me explain further.

Try to remain active and energized during this phase. I suggest selecting three to five individuals to assist you. I further recommend you pick people from both your personal and professional lives. It is also really important that you choose not only people you think know you quite well, but also people who may not be as familiar with you. Their impressions may be different and perhaps not as well-founded as those who know you better, but initial impressions can be so meaningful. Try your best to include them to an extent you feel appropriate.

It is also important that you include in your list individuals who approach things very differently from you—people who perhaps don't quite line up with your way of thinking. This diversity of thought is so important because what you are looking for are people to tell you what you need to know, not what you want to hear. There is a huge difference.

Once you have your list, contact each person individually and explain to him or her what you are doing and why you are doing it. Go over the process with each person so your expectations are clear. Let them know you want their insight! In spite of the guidance I have offered here to make my point and to be instructive, please work hard to keep any unnecessary formality from creeping in. Remember, the purpose is simply to get perspectives from others.

I want to help by offering you the following reminders as you seek out, receive, and study the feedback you acquire during the exercise above:

Seek out all you need to know with a vengeance.

- ⊃ *You must practice active listening.* It will be close to impossible for you to understand what someone is telling you and equally unlikely for you to gain the benefit of that insight if you're really not listening to them. If you find yourself drifting in thought or beginning to defend your beliefs, stop and listen!

- ⊃ *Do not be defensive.* You may want to defend a behavior or trait one of your interviewees has identified. Don't go there. You do not want to discourage other individuals from being open and honest. This is a huge pitfall that you must work hard to avoid! I'm still working on this; I find it one of my biggest challenges. If you do so, others will likely shut down, and if that occurs, you've missed out on the opportunity to gain their insights. What a loss that would be!

- *Do all you can to encourage them.* Thank them for their insight and show your appreciation. Always be completely sincere.

- *Ask carefully for clarification.* You need to have a clear understanding of exactly what they are saying to you. This is very important; yet, keep in mind this is where you may tend to defend your behavior. Be aware of this!

Once you have gathered all the feedback, organized it in a way that will benefit you, and understand the inputs thoroughly, take some time to reflect on all you have learned. Study the information you have received carefully and thoroughly. Make some comparisons on the feedback with your self-assessment. Look at the common areas as perhaps validations of their relevance, but pay equal, if not more attention, to those areas that are different. Do not fall into the trap of discounting or eliminating them as inaccurate! Dig deep and see if you can relate to what others have said, and see how these behaviors may manifest. Keep them as constant reminders of what someone else sees in you.

Perhaps, because I have talked about it throughout this entire chapter, you will simply overlook the significance of the effort you will expend in examining yourself this way. In looking in the mirror, you may draw the conclusion that what you see is adequate, and if you feel that way it's fine. Others may look in the mirror, and what they see is all they may ever become. The magic here is whether you accept that as finality, as reality with an outcome set in stone. Or does the concept of becoming more—something far more—intrigue you and excite you to become more self-aware and to explore the possibilities of what might lie ahead? I believe one of life's biggest mistakes is not having the interest, the courage, or the respect for ourselves at least to explore this question a bit more.

The easiest and initial part of your professional and personal planning is now complete. It's time for you now to make a commitment through your follow-up actions to yourself first then to all those who have helped you so far. What are you going to do with all that you have learned?

Self-Assessment: Sample Skill Set Checklist

SKILL	DEFINITION OR EXAMPLE	CURRENT SKILL LEVEL (1–10)	DEGREE OF IMPORTANCE Current (1–10)	Future (1–10)
Example:				
Visionary	The ability to think long-term	1	3	10
Energetic	The ability to demonstrate excitement	4	6	10
Passionate	To exhibit a deep sense of caring	4	6	10
Confident	Demonstrating self-assurance	8	7	10
Other		-		

Notes:

➲ Use this checklist to both identify and define your individual skills. You can also use it to add skills over time to others that are similar, grouping them into sets (like "energetic," "passionate," "confident," etc.).

➲ You may list skills you are good at, ones you enjoy and practice, and others you do not enjoy but possess, and so on.

➲ You can list skills that are of interest to you or that you find are necessary regardless of whether you possess them or not.

➲ Assign a relative strength to both the skill and its importance to you currently and in the future (e.g., 1–10 in increasing capability or importance).

➲ A list of actions will naturally follow your skill needs.

List of Actions

<u>**Example:**</u>

Visionary:

- ➲ Try to think in the longer-term as a first step.

  Note: To improve the effectiveness of your plan, include specific dates for the initiation and completion of each action.

- ➲ Participate in a strategic planning process for the fiscal year. Include specific dates for each action.

- ➲ Get exposure to a business development organization to gain long-term planning experience.

- ➲ Work in advanced technology to get a sense of long-term technology trends.

- ➲ Get involved with challenges that stretch your comfort levels and invigorate you.

CHAPTER 2

THE STARTING LINE

You have made a commitment to yourself to take control of your development and accept accountability for the results. You took an initial big step in creating your career development plan by looking in the mirror and taking into account what you saw. Furthermore, you validated and complemented a self-assessment and reached out to a diverse set of personal and professional individuals in your life to gain additional perspectives.

I remember that when I first initiated this planning discipline effort for myself, it came off as very administrative, dry, and lacking excitement. What I found early on was quite valid, particularly during the formative stages of the process. But my attitude and energy levels soared once the implementation of the plan began to yield results. It fired me up and fueled my energy to place even more emphasis on the plan over time. The same will happen to you in time if you give it a chance!

Collecting, organizing, and analyzing the feedback you now possess will give you an initial yet comprehensive list of your skill strengths, areas for improvement, likes, and dislikes. In addition, you have made another firm and important commitment to do something with the information you now have. Everyone wants to be a winner, but not everyone has the energy or desire to do what it takes. Don't forget the need to remain unwavering in the commitment you made to yourself in spite of the challenges and hard work that remain ahead. You need to prepare in order to win. You have to start somewhere, and I want to give you several things to think about as you begin to formulate your plan.

If you look at all the successful organizations, from the top Fortune 500 corporations to single-employee small businesses, there is a constant element that is critical to their continued success: the presence of a living, evolving strategic and financial plan. Important elements in such a plan usually include a market outlook, competitive dynamics, key product/service differentiators, innovative technologies, discretionary and capital investments, revenue and margin commitments, human resource needs, and so on. It is essential that each and every action, goal, objective, and commitment within any plan is tied back to an individual or set of objectives defined in the plan. These objectives are normally longer-term (five to ten years) and are continuous and ever evolving. The very real possibility that the business's focus will evolve over time enables the organization and the individuals within it to achieve the established vision because the plan is a living document and alterations to the plan are inevitable.

My point is simple but at the same time so pertinent: you need to look at both your personal development and your professional development *in the same way*! One of the most common questions is: What do I want to do with my life? We've all been asked this by those closest to us, and we've asked the same thing of ourselves and of others. For some the question came early in life, and the answer may or may not have been clear. The most important aspect here is that at some point, we—particularly those of us whose personal and professional purposes are not clear—must spend quality time trying to understand this to a much greater extent.

The point is that regardless of where you are on that spectrum, we all have to start somewhere. In my case, I initially wanted to be the best individual contributing engineer. But soon after the ink was dry on that objective, my long-term objectives changed. At that point I began to learn, develop, and practice my concept of career planning because it just wouldn't exist otherwise. This is not in any way a criticism of my employer or my leader at the time; it was my coming to that realization that energized me to take control of my destiny. I needed to take charge! For all of us, it really is not important where we start because we can start anywhere. What is important is what we do with all we have learned about ourselves in addition to what our evolving thoughts may reveal to us about what we want to become. Defining who you are and what you want to be must occur before determining what you want to do when you grow up. That is the key.

I want you to think about the following as you begin this next step. First, do not give credence to any self-imposed limitations you may have created. I have heard them all from people I've mentored and led. Statements like, "I just don't see that happening to me," "I'm just not that lucky," "I'm not capable," and "I can't see myself achieving that level of success," are all too common. These are self-created fallacies, and, in many cases, without any real basis. Thinking like this will severely limit your self-worth and directly impact any energy you will have left with which to act.

We all waste a tremendous amount of time making excuses for why something won't or can't occur. My initial limitation was that I didn't—or wouldn't—think that far ahead; the concept of becoming chief operating officer had not yet even entered my mind at that point. On top of that, I incorrectly drew the conclusion that a person from the Northeast didn't fit well in the Midwest environment. No one told me this, you see. I created these ghosts myself. Initially this impeded my thinking and stunted my growth as a person and a professional. That would soon change; but when I look back to that time, I now realize that a more positive approach should have started with another question: Why not me? That's right—why not you? We all have to step up to the starting line sometime, and there's no better time than now. This applies to anything you aspire to in all aspects of your life.

Now, take a good hard look at your initial assessment. What is it telling you about yourself? Equally important, what does it not say about you? Keep these thoughts in the back of your mind as you try to define what your personal and professional endgames are. The earlier in your life you try to do so, the more difficult answering this question becomes. At the same time, this will provide you more time to develop a higher-quality development plan.

If you can simply imagine big things for yourself, you are one step closer to making them a reality.

You need to start this process early—in fact, start now! Pick a handful of long-term objectives and try to imagine yourself in each of those situations without limitations. Think about how interesting each of them is to you: What excites you most? What fires you up? What can you get the most passionate about? Only you have the answers to these questions—no one else but you! Thinking about how passionate you are about each life opportunity will allow you to visualize to what extent each option will challenge and energize you. This will enable you to think about where you can learn the most, how you can have some fun, and how you can best make the biggest difference.

I get fired up about many things, and I always find they relate back to my ability to learn, have fun, and make a difference each and every day. I have also noticed that the significance of each of these criteria isn't as important to me as the fact that I address and satisfy them in some fashion. Helping an employee deal with a work-related or personal issue gives me tremendous energy. Dealing with dissatisfied customers and converting them to personal and corporate advocates incites me to do more. Like I said, those three criteria are key for me! I am confident if you embrace them as I have done, they will be just as impactful for you.

You should make a point to go back to your self-assessment continuously and outline what skill sets you really enjoy applying, define those you prefer not to focus on, and add emphasis to the skill sets you feel require further development.

When it is all said and done, how and what you spend your professional development time on should be based on your long-term objectives, your skill set needs, and capitalizing on attributes you either enjoy or prefer to avoid.

I recommend you ask yourself a series of very important questions. On the surface, depending on where you are in your personal and professional maturity, the answers to these questions may not seem all that critical. In determining the quality of your professional life, the answers are quite instrumental. These questions are:

- ⮑ What is my timeline for accomplishing certain objectives in my life?

- ⮑ At what point in my journey do I want to achieve a certain set of developmental objectives?

- ⮑ Where do I see myself at the end of my career?

- ⮑ What legacy will I leave behind?

A goal without a timeline to measure progress against, is a goal that anyone will be challenged to achieve. Don't treat this as an exact science; I encourage you to take an educated guess at first. Let me share with you how I approached this for my development plan.

As I mentioned earlier, I will continually refer to the three things I see as most important in deciding what I want to spend my life doing. In every aspect of my life, it's important that I enjoy what I'm doing. Enjoyment for me comes in many forms, such as challenge, failure, success, progress, stress, creativity, problem solving, decision making, and the like. I have fun dealing with all that comes my way as long as it's accompanied by learning something new each and every day. I have to feel I am better off for having spent time learning through every opportunity.

It is equally important for me to have made a difference after having decided to spend my time and energy on something. Otherwise there is no value or true contribution that comes from my efforts. This "effort for no value" scenario doesn't align at all with my life's purpose. I think you will find that by embracing these three criteria, your approach and attitude toward making the best use of your time will take on a whole new meaning. I truly believe that.

I began to notice in my professional career that after a few years in any role, one or more of these three satisfaction criteria were waning. Since I really didn't embrace a career planning discipline until a few years into my career, I applied this learning moving forward into my career planning process. I established a timeline for each future role based on the thoughts that my

> *Learn, have fun, and make a difference each and every day.*

enthusiasm and effectiveness in my current role would begin to weaken in two-and-a-half to three years. This assumption served many purposes for me. First, it kept me energized in my role, and it helped me strive for and seek out the more challenging assignments continuously. This in turn did wonders for boosting my level of accomplishment. It also gave me objectives to shoot for regardless of whether or not they actually turned out exactly as planned. That aspect was not crucial, but it was important. It also encouraged me to keep an eye out for that next opportunity to make a difference without compromising my commitment to my current focus. That was highly energizing to me. Thinking about what could be next for me without compromising my focus on the present day's commitments was exciting!

Each position along the way would initially offer me a renewed sense of purpose, an opportunity to learn new skills and to make some form of difference. But when one or more of the criteria became fully satisfied, I would clearly notice that my passion and energy for the role would begin to wane. It happened that way quite frequently. The solutions to issues became common and required less creativity on my part. Or I didn't feel enough challenge or stretch in my assignments. That all would translate quite quickly into impacting my satisfaction levels in whatever I was doing.

Interestingly enough, in more than thirty years with one employer, I had thirteen different roles. Some lasted as short as ten months; the longest I spent in any role before moving on was four years. The math would tell you I spent a little more than two years in each role. That was not far off from the premise I established and shared with you earlier. I progressed from an entry-level design engineer to chief operating officer of the company over a twenty-year time frame. My journey along the way included roles in engineering, product management, business development, and marketing and sales. With each new challenge came the opportunity to add additional skills, gain a diverse set of experiences, and make real differences. I spent my final ten years as the operating officer in multiple businesses within the company. Think about where I came from and know that this can happen to you if it is what you choose. However, no matter what your end objective may be, achieving it can happen only if you don't accept mediocrity as an option and are willing to do all it takes to prepare yourself for success.

Let's look at a few other variables to think about as you decide how, where, and what you want to spend your time on as you attempt to live your life to the fullest. While some may be obvious, others are a bit less evident, but the degree of importance they play in your fulfillment remains significant. Let me go through a few that come to mind.

Consider whether you have any geographical restrictions or any aspirations to gain some of life's experiences in diverse domestic and international locations. Is where you reside important to you? If you spend just eight hours a day in some role, you are spending the remaining sixteen hours doing something other than work. It goes without saying that it would be better for you to be in a location for which you have some affinity.

Are there certain potential-employer attributes that are important to you? Do you value a larger, more diverse corporate environment, or do you prefer a smaller, more focused work environment? Does the concept of being an entrepreneur excite you? There are a series of pros and cons to each alternative. It's important for you to assess each opportunity on its own set of merits. Keep in mind that you are looking for what fires you up, what you can see yourself doing, and something about which you can be highly passionate. Most important, how can you learn, have fun, and make a difference every day?

Staying with your professional development, I also suggest you spend some time thinking about the core values that are important to you and whether or not a current or prospective employer and/or industry treats those same values as passionately as you do. If I look back in time at the earliest stages of my career after college, I recall what was most important to me then. I put an emphasis on expanding my geographical horizons during my pre graduation job interview process. I chose to relocate to the Midwest from the Northeast as I wanted a change in venue. I wanted to experience a different pace of life. I chose to explore career opportunities that would get me away from the comfort of my current surroundings. Going to work for an organization that offered the opportunity for long-term stability was important to me. Benefits such as a 401(k), a retirement plan, robust health care benefits, and reasonable vacation and holiday policies were significant to me as well. What was in the back of my mind at the time, but not yet a priority, was working in an environment that best provided me the opportunity to excel! However, what became vital to me over time—though I didn't realize it until it occurred—was how a prospective employer valued its people.

I was interviewing at the company with which I would eventually spend my entire career. The president of the company at the time made it a point to greet each incoming group of recruits. At my visit, he welcomed us each individually. What was even more powerful was that he spent some time getting to know each of us. He was the president of a large corporation, yet he so valued the importance of the recruitment and selection process of employees to the success of his company, he made it a priority.

Six months after that interview, I began my career at the company. On my first day, I met the same president again, and he remembered my name and a few other pertinent personal facts about my life and me. I must tell you, in all the other interviews I'd had while searching for my initial employment opportunity, I had never met with any other corporate executives or members of senior leadership. At most my exposure had been limited to recruiting representatives from human resources departments and members of the specific organizations with whom I was interviewing. You see, I made a huge life decision by placing a large amount of emphasis on things that were important to me. I wanted to work at a place where people were not only viewed as important but also treated like they were! That particular president's attitude toward how much value he placed on people sealed the deal for me. I spent my entire professional career at that company and never resented it for a single minute.

I'm not saying this exact scenario is right for your particular situation, but the concept of placing the right amount of emphasis on what's important when making huge choices in life applies to each of us, in all aspects of our lives.

Regardless of your career aspirations, I am going to challenge you to do some research on what prospective employers are looking for as they assess potential employees. This all applies whether you are at an entry-level position or you are a more seasoned veteran looking to reenergize your career. As you address this challenge, you will find that the infinite variety of employers and industries available to you makes it complex. As a result, there is no one common and complete response to this challenge. What is important to you should always be at the top of your list.

Never compromise your values or anything you deem critical.

I am continually asked about what employers look for when they interview people for roles, aside from the obvious hard skills. For starters, I am always under the assumption that when you walk in the room to have a dialogue with me, you possess the basic technical, job-related hard skills necessary to execute the responsibilities of the position. Or, at a minimum, you possess the near-term potential to be highly effective and competent. I consider these hard skills to be table stakes for the most part. What I really look for is any tangible evidence that you recognize the importance of the skill sets, attributes, and values that some people would define as the *soft* skills. These are related to personal attributes that enhance an individual's ability to interact with others. We will discuss these skills in far more detail later, but for the purpose of demonstrating this point, let me offer these questions for you to ponder:

- ➲ Do you have good listening skills? You can't learn from others if you don't listen to them.

- ➲ Do you have any evidence of doing what you say you will do, of consistently fulfilling commitments? It doesn't matter what it is specifically, but if you have made a commitment, you need to do what you say you will do to make it right.

- ➲ Are you passionate about your personal and professional lives? Energy is contagious.

- ➲ Do you think about things in deeper and more complex ways? Thinking beyond the obvious implies creativity.

- ➲ Do you practice true diversity, and can you excel in a collaborative environment? To compete in any aspect of life, you must differentiate, and what better way to do that than through a highly collaborative, diverse team of talented professionals?

➲ Have you given some thought to what is important to you in your life and your career?

➲ Are you active in your personal and professional communities? Possessing a wide and deep network as well as the drive to give back is important; I always look for high-performance talent.

As I've said, the keystone of career planning is taking ownership of your career and life—leading your own way! This applies to every aspect of your life. The questions above not only relate directly to several key attributes of a leader but are important in your individual development.

I am all about hiring current and potential leadership for any position, just as I am all about choosing my personal network and populating it with people who can make each other better. In other words, I want to fill my company and my life with diverse individuals who are energized about who they are and what they want to accomplish. I am looking for people who respect the perspectives of others and are motivated to collaborate with each other to create outcomes that will excite those around us. Also, having a team or a personal network of individuals who consistently demonstrate compliant and ethical delivery on commitments is of utmost importance to me.

All of us are equipped with capabilities and competencies that are varied in type and level. As we continue our journey, I ask you to use your strengths as the foundation of your approach but also to spend more than your fair share of time identifying and developing those skill shortcomings that you know are important to you. Chapters three, four, and five will offer you some perspectives on how to go about doing that.

Those who know me would describe me as a highly passionate individual. They would add that I am passionate about everything I do and that I seem to possess unlimited energy. I am sure some would go on to say I am a bit intimidating on first impression, and I have quite a driven personality with a generous side that borders on excessive. My direct but honest nature would make the list as well.

What they likely won't say, because most don't know it, is that the impetus behind my character comes from that day in the driveway with my father when he told me I could become so much more, and if I did all I could do, my time on Earth would be filled with so many rewarding experiences. To use a baseball analogy, when I make the final run around the bases and head for home, I want to slide into home plate having spent all my energy and having not one regret about how I played the game.

You've looked in the mirror and started down the path of creating your professional legacy. The process is just beginning. I want to remind you once again that this is an art, not an exact science. If done correctly, this process is never ending; you will continue it until the day you stop learning. You will find you may have to take a step back now to take a step forward later. Do not succumb to mediocrity or an assumed lack of progress. Instead use any feeling of stagnation you may be experiencing to drive you to action. Do not accept anything less from yourself, ever. Mediocrity is not an option.

Our lives are relatively short. If we are lucky enough to reach the average life expectancy, it still does not compare to the time that has elapsed since the creation of the universe. However, it is the time we have, and to that end, it is a significant gift. There are no

With no promises for tomorrow, make today count!

promises for tomorrow. To me it's what you are going to do today and every other day you have been given to make the most of your time here. The way you live is your gift to yourself and to those around you. Don't waste a single minute or pass up an opportunity to make your life truly fantastic. Accepting mediocrity is disrespectful to the time with which we have been blessed.

CHAPTER 3

ADDING MENTORS TO THE MIX

We are at the point in our journey where I will strongly encourage you to take your planning to a new level. I am now going to help you learn how to expand your perspective. I'll ask you to go beyond including just what you know and what others think they know and include perspectives from those who do know! There is a monumental difference.

I now want to take some time to introduce a very important, powerful leadership and career development tool. It's called mentoring.

If you understand the basic concept of mentorship, that is a good start. If you don't, do not be concerned because you will understand it soon enough. We can trace the concept of mentoring back to Greek roots. Since that time the model has evolved, its importance has varied, and its application has taken on broader meaning. The terms *peer, coach, counselor,* and *guide* were developed over time and have taken on new meanings along with expanded roles.

The practice of a person learning from others has a long and varied history, but the basic concepts still apply across many vocations. Trades such as electrical and plumbing contracting were founded on the model of completing apprenticeships to reach increased levels of competency. Other professional examples of this are medical residencies and engineering internships. A surgeon does not learn how to remove tonsils or perform an appendectomy by simply reading about it in a medical textbook. While certainly a book would introduce the process steps and protocols, surgeons will tell you they developed their expertise by actually performing these procedures with mentors, as in subject matter experts, overseeing and guiding them, refining their techniques with each new experience. Never underestimate the importance of learning in a one-on-one, hands-on arrangement.

The impact that electronic media has had on people's general attitude toward mentoring has been significant. From my vantage point, the increased use of social networking has taken away from people's willingness—and maybe even more so their ability—to sit down and converse.

> *Passing on one's personal and professional experiences to others is invaluable.*

The convenience of being able to chat with anyone, anywhere, at any time has greatly influenced people's affinity for and ability to have direct, complex, and meaningful dialogues with one another. Of course there are exceptions, but I simply ask you to look around and observe people's behaviors. Many of us are on our phones even while we are in direct conversations with others! That's just the way it is.

In order for this powerful development tool—mentoring—to be most effective, we need to have far more direct and meaningful conversations. I'm not asking you to toss your smartphone, I am simply suggesting that conversations about important things need to take place and take place as directly as possible.

Let's define just what a mentor is within the big picture. I define a mentor as one who willingly dedicates his or her time to sharing personal and professional experiences with another. Furthermore, mentors will take the time necessary to understand as much as they can about the individuals seeking guidance (the mentees) and can anticipate what they seek. Sometimes it is obvious, but in many cases it's not. This is particularly valid when you are dealing with things like cultural or generational differences between the mentor and mentee.

This is vitally important because the effectiveness of the relationship improves greatly when the mentor knows or strongly senses what is truly on the mind of the mentee. It is then important that the mentor keeps that at the very forefront of the dialogue as he or she shares experiences and offers guidance. I can recall so many instances in which the simple act of making time for someone was so significant in that person's eyes. Then to be able to listen, to help that person think through challenges, and provide some guidance on a way forward is invigorating for all involved. The needs of the mentee must be the focus.

Let's discuss some things that may likely be running through your mind—things like: How do I make this happen? Does this process need to be formal? Can a more casual relationship be effective? I'm not part of a large organization, and my access to people who can help is limited. What do I look for, and how do I go about finding a mentor?

Let's address the most significant question first: How do I make this happen? I can offer you some practical advice. First, ask yourself what you really want to accomplish and what your primary objective is. The answer to this will help you further define the specific type of person and expertise that will be of most help to you. Second, if your organization has a mentoring program, find a way to get involved. This may take some effort, but you must persist. Whether this exists or not, look outside your professional domain as mentors can be prevalent in every aspect of our lives. Third, make sure you have enough information about what you want to accomplish because the mentors you seek may have many demands on their time. You must try to differentiate yourself as much as possible to help the mentor draw the conclusion that spending time with you will be of greater value then spending their time elsewhere.

Fourth, be very specific about your expectations and what you want from your mentors. Finally, be prepared to reciprocate and offer them feedback if called upon to do so. If you are willing to avail your time for the benefit of others, the process of finding mentors will become much clearer and more effective. In the end you have to look at this process of learning more about yourself and what the possibilities are for you as fun, exciting, and a highly valuable way to spend your time!

Now, with respect to the level of formality that is required here, the truth is that unlike formal mentoring programs that exist both in person and online, the informal variety can just happen—similar to the discussion I had with my dentist that I discussed in the introduction to this book. That dialogue came about because one or both of us saw a need, and there was a willingness to engage. There were no scheduling or other logistics to consider. It was simply two individuals who came together, and the opportunity to share ideas and learn just happened. I can say without reservation that while one acted primarily as mentor and the other as mentee, we both learned and taught each other something.

There are huge differences between formal and informal mentoring relationships, and I feel this warrants a brief discussion because, in the end, you will have to decide what is best for you and what may be possible given your current situation. One size does not fit all here, and it's important that you understand there is flexibility and that you have options. Let me highlight some of the more substantial characteristics:

- ➲ Formality implies expectations. Mutual expectations must be clear from the start; if they're not, you are wasting time. This does not really come into play in the more casual model.

- ➲ Others in your network or sphere of influence can view formality as threatening. The threat manifests through the insecurities of those who don't participate in something similar. I suggest you deal with this by treating the process with the respect we discussed, and don't let others' insecurities dissuade you. It's difficult enough to manage yourself through this process, let alone deal with the dynamics of others whose intentions are unclear.

- ➲ In some ways, formality encourages those without the social skills to engage informally to participate. I don't see an issue with this, but this type of mentee likely will need more encouragement and confidence from the mentor. In this case, the mentor will need to take on a more proactive role.

- ➲ Formality implies "arranged." Chemistry is crucial and is more of a natural outcome with informality.

⮂   Trust is a very important component regardless of the level of formality. It's usually easier to develop using the informal model.

I have had the honor of having several mentors throughout my life; they were present and important in all aspects of both the personal and professional realms. While some were more effective than others, each and every one of them was in some way instrumental to my development.

One of the most effective formal mentors came into my professional life in the latter stages of my career. He became my direct leader as our chief executive officer when I first became a chief operating officer. Right from the beginning, I knew we were alike in many ways, yet it was apparent we were also quite different in equally as many ways. My background was more in operational excellence and performance related, while he was clearly a bigger-picture visionary. Over time we learned a great deal from one another.

What I remember most is that he was one of the very few mentors who focused on my areas that required improvement and on what I needed to do to reach my full potential. We spent very little time on my skill strengths because our mutual purpose was to help me become all I was capable of becoming. Yes, it was very difficult at times to listen to what he had to say, but he was telling me what I needed to know and not what I wanted to hear. His impact on my development was significant, but along with that progression came a lot of complex and difficult conversations that were both necessary and had great impact.

I remember each and every one of our development-related conversations, but the one that sticks with me most was our very first one. I entered the room not expecting to focus on my shortcomings, but that was really all we talked about. My need to be a better listener, to look more at the big picture, and to be more cognizant of my body language all came up. I left there a bit uptight because it all had come unexpectedly. But he hadn't told me anything I didn't already know. The difference was that he felt it was important for me to address the issues, and he took the time and responsibility to motivate me to improve. That's the true role of any leader!

Both approaches can work and be effective. It's really up to you to decide which approach you choose and just how much you want to invest in your development. Remember, nothing great comes easily, so don't let the difficulty factor dissuade you. In the end, mentoring is all about honoring and respecting the human resource in all aspects of our lives. Something special occurs when people reach deep inside to bring out the best in each other.

Now, let's examine several of the most essential mentor traits we should consider when we get to the point where seeking one out is upon us.

Credibility

It is important that anyone you are considering as a mentor has credibility. What you are looking for is an individual who is recognized as one who possesses and has successfully applied the specific skills you are seeking to develop within yourself. There is nothing quite like hearing from those who have "been there and done that" successfully to jump-start your development.

Willingness

I have found, regardless of whether or not there is a formal mentoring program available, finding a credible individual who understands the value of serving as someone's mentor is crucial to the effectiveness of the interaction. When I mentor I'm all in. I get prepared in advance. I consider serving in this capacity as a huge responsibility and honor. I very rarely cancel or postpone. I have a set of objectives I intend on achieving, and I become energized in the process. You must find someone who sees and believes in the value of the experience. I always look forward to these conversations as they satisfy my strong desire to give back and make a difference in others' lives.

Focus

This next characteristic is related to willingness but at the same time different enough to warrant its own mention. That is, the ability to focus and stay in the moment. It is so easy to become distracted by personal or business issues, texts and other messages, e-mails, phone calls, or any other of a long list of interruptions. Look for a mentor who has the ability to stay in the moment. The effectiveness of your dialogue will increase, and the signal such a mentor sends is such a positive reinforcement of his or her commitment to both you and the process.

Communication Skills

Let's talk about being an effective communicator. Usually, getting someone to share his or her experiences and personal perspectives is not the most significant challenge you will face when looking for a mentor. However, finding someone who is capable and can consistently be an active listener is usually the more substantial hurdle to overcome. It is almost impossible for someone to get a feel for your needs, concerns, and objectives—let alone achieve mutual trust and confidence—if he or she can't listen.

This has always been a challenge for me. My enthusiasm, energy, and excitement rise in the process of helping someone, and sometimes have me talking far more than I am listening. Over time, and with the help of my mentors, leadership, friends, family, business associates, and others, I have made vast improvements in this area. Nonetheless, it remains a challenge for me to this day!

Accessibility

Picking a mentor who will make the time to converse with the appropriate degree of regularity will keep the process energized as you move forward. It is easy for some to put this off or treat it with less than its deserved level of importance. So be mindful of this when seeking out your mentors.

Practice the art of active listening.

Constructive Criticism

Now, let's talk about your mentors' ability to be critical yet constructive. We talked about the need to keep an open mind, to listen, and not to become defensive when receiving feedback. Those principles apply during the mentoring process. You want to find mentors who will be direct and talk about the skills and behaviors you may need to work on more; who will tell you what you need to know in a manner that is always respectful and honest. Remember, at the same time you will need to continue to be a great listener.

Teaching Ability

A mentor needs to be instructive and always the teacher. This is a very important quality because your primary objective as a mentee is to learn! This capability facilitates the open sharing of both personal and professional experiences that are applicable to the topic under discussion. This is also the quality that provides the mentor with an opportunity to share his or her insights and situational perspectives. Perhaps this would also include a discussion of some of the mentor's biggest challenges and most difficult decisions. Things that worked out and things that did not go as planned are both important points of discussion. Mentoring is all about learning from the experiences of others.

Please understand that there is a fine line between offering guidance and telling someone what to do. Sometimes the mentee is looking for one or the other, but in my view mentees should select mentors who are great advisers and try to steer away from those who are going to make the decisions for them. Remember, your development is your responsibility. If you find yourself in this position, I encourage you to take advantage of all the information, guidance, advice, and perspectives offered up, but in the end it is up to you to decide what's next. You need to go into this process not looking to be told what to do. That's what taking control of your destiny is all about!

I have a very close friend who is the owner of a very successful small business. As in any business, there is always room for improvement. He has gotten to know me quite well over the past few years, and in parallel, I have earned his respect and he has earned mine. At times he has sought out my perspectives when dealing with personal and professional challenges that normally come with operating a business. He is extremely competent and highly accredited in his professional domains and has made the commitment to learn more about leadership to improve his effectiveness and the performance of his business. When he seeks my guidance, there are times when we land on very different sides of how to deal with an issue. This is quite natural, and it happens all the time. I am more proactive and direct while he is a bit more indirect, reflective, and less confrontational.

As you can imagine, this has set the stage for some very interesting discussions. Sometimes, when listening to him describe a situation, I have found myself taking control of the dialogue, cutting to the chase, and defining what he should do. At times I would even catch myself saying, "Done, next," when I was ready to move on in the dialogue, not even considering where his mind was. When I first did that, he simply shut down and let me continue on to my conclusion. But after some time, as our relationship grew, he became more comfortable with telling me not to go there. He truly appreciated the guidance, and we both knew the ultimate decisions on what to do and when to act rested with him. When he thanked me for my advice, I knew he was also telling me not to tell him specifically what to do.

The lesson here is that, where possible, you need to get to a point in the mentor-mentee relationship where you know each other well, your roles are well understood, and you can both open up to make the relationship as mutually beneficial as possible. You both can teach and learn so much from each other at the same time if you let yourselves!

The mentoring world can be filled with diversion, avoidance, and a lack of specificity. Seek out individuals who do not avoid talking about reality, who are direct and to the point, and who are not at all inhibited about openly sharing their knowledge. You will learn a great deal more when you are both able to discuss openly things that didn't go quite right. This brings a sense of credibility to the mentor-mentee relationship that will serve both sides quite well over the longer-term.

Critical Thinking

You will want to find a mentor who practices the art of critical thinking. One's ability to probe deeply and not waste time on the obvious will improve the quality and effectiveness of your conversations. When your mentor asks you to think about things in a different and deeper way, an improved outcome will result. You will notice as you prepare that your attention to detail and diversity of thought will improve because you know what he or she expects of you. Expectations drive actions, which in turn improve both the quality of the results and your chances of success.

One final thought on this trait: your mentor should surprise you somehow in each conversation with unique perspectives that get your creativity flowing. This is yet another way to push out mediocrity.

Objectivity

This is the last significant mentor trait warranting mention. It refers to the mentor's ability to take the high road, to stay positive, energetic, and upbeat. The shadow of leadership looms large here. A mentor who demonstrates a positive, can-do passion for life will go a long way toward breaking down the many barriers to learning in the process that may exist.

Now, I know what you may be saying to yourself right now: Where am I going to find a mentor who possesses all or most of these traits? Or even further, if he or she does exist, why would this person want to mentor me? To this I offer a couple of thoughts. First, these individuals do exist, and if they are truly well-rounded or true leaders in any setting, they will possess many of the tools necessary to serve as highly effective mentors to you.

As both a friend and a leader, I mentored thousands of aspiring individuals throughout my life; my mentoring door was open to everyone. As I have already said, possessing the willingness and energy to make a real difference in someone's life is critical. In the event that you can't find that one mentor who has everything you're looking for, I have found that having more than one can be quite useful, particularly when trying to seek out diverse perspectives. The primary challenge in this is your ability to manage multiple relationships. While having more than one mentor poses challenges, the benefits can be significant. These individuals exist, and they are all around you in every aspect of your life. You need to seek them out actively in whatever way you can to have the best chance at success. This takes some effort, and you must be persistent.

I think it's really important to talk now about the possibility that availability or access to a mentor for you is still problematic. Perhaps you are new to an area or an organization, and you have not yet established a network. Or, as mentioned earlier, your professional environment does not offer a formal mentor-mentee program for you to use. Maybe your personal network has been impacted in some way so that it now needs to be enhanced. For those of you in this situation, all hope is not lost. I truly prefer face-to-face, more personal types of mentor relationships, but if that's not possible or practical there are online options for those whose situations warrant them or for those who prefer to go that route for this part of their planning.

There are many services to introduce and assist those in search of online mentor-mentee tools. Many of these platforms apply workplace science and technology data in a tool that, if applicable, can effectively help people with their development needs. Some of the less robust tools simply offer general guidance on how to focus and develop specific skills. Others offer far more elaborate and effective tools that provide seamless online mentor-mentee experiences without your ever having to leave your computer. Regardless of the method or tools you choose, this book is all about your taking on the responsibility for leading your personal and professional career development and giving you a sense of direction on how to go about getting that accomplished.

If you find yourself in the situation where learning more about what these on-line tools are all about and what they may offer you, I encourage you to use your favorite search engine. By using key words such as mentor-mentee relationships and mentor-mentee processes, you will quickly be offered a myriad of opportunities to learn more about how an on-line service may be helpful to you. I worked hard to put myself in positions where the more personal and direct form of this type of relationship was realistic for me because I felt it was important. You can do exactly the same thing if it's what you want. The choice is yours and the good news is that you have options.

I want to reiterate my strong belief that taking a proactive approach in seeking out mentors who can and will support direct relationships will result in highly effective outcomes. However, if you find that won't work for you, you have other options to consider. Simply remember that this part of the process takes a tremendous amount of self-direction, energy, and time. It's far easier to say it's too difficult and avoid it all together. I have seen this occur more times than I care to mention, and to that I say, what a huge loss!

CHAPTER 4

BECOME A MENTEE: LEAD THE WAY

We have discussed the mentoring process, and I have described the most essential traits of a mentor and offered some guidance on how to find one. Now, let's switch gears and talk at length about *your* roles and responsibilities as a mentee. I am going to continue on with my premise that you will use a combination of both the formal and informal approaches to the mentor-mentee process simply because my experiences have taught me this is the most likely and impactful way ahead. This is an area where you will have complete control over your attitude, actions, decisions, preparedness, and the like. We are now beginning to move further toward the action/building commitment stages of the planning process. What follows are some additional things to take into consideration as you prepare to do your part in developing and nurturing the mentor-mentee relationship.

Familiarization

The most important initial step for you as a mentee is to familiarize yourself with your proposed mentor(s). Do all you can to become familiar with his or her values and attributes. Also there is a lot to be gained by getting a better understanding of some of the more significant projects or efforts in which your mentor played a large role. The better you can understand his or her operating style or model, the more substantial your discussions and ensuing relationship will become. I can assure you the mentor will bring up what you have learned as a part of your interchanges, and your advanced familiarity with what is being discussed will serve you well. Do your mentor homework in advance!

Being All In

Next, I want you to give this process all the time and energy it warrants. Stay focused on this important part of your development. You need to keep in mind that your mentor will likely have a full-time job as well as a personal life. To serve actively and effectively as a mentor, he or she will be spending significant time and attention away from both and dedicating his or her energy to you and this process. The most effective ways to demonstrate your personal commitment to the process is to be focused, prepared, and to show your appreciation. I cannot tell you the number of mentees I have partnered with who came late, unprepared, and clearly not expecting to invest the time and energy necessary to make the relationship work. While some of them gave up, many more learned, grew, and accepted my challenges. In some cases my mentees were friends, associates, and professionals who understood and clearly accepted their roles in their own personal development.

I need to underscore the importance of staying in the process, working the relationship, and making the time available. Be patient. I recognize that most people say they are busy, but that's the usual excuse they offer up when it comes to dealing with processes such as this. The more tactical or shorter-term demands on our time often take precedence over something more strategic or longer-term in nature. Make the time! Keep in mind that the mentor-mentee relationship, like any other partnership, takes time to develop and evolve into something special. But with time, patience, persistence, and action, the effort will serve you well in the longer-term. Trust me.

Balance

Let me offer a few additional ideas to keep in mind as you prepare to select and eventually engage with your mentor. While diverse cultural, generational, and personality aspects may be at play in some cases, work to find a balance between pushing too hard and being too direct with being too passive and evasive. This is a challenge for many, and the chemistry between the parties will form the foundation to help this work its way out. Be mindful of the dynamic.

Also, with all the electronic media available today, take advantage of it and use it as a tool to stay connected. As I have noted, it is not a substitute for face-to-face dialogue. Turn off your phone while you are with your mentor, and stay in the moment. Remember that your actions speak louder than your words.

One way to determine the level of interest in or importance given to the process is for both parties to assess the quality of the required follow-up activity or action plan. People normally take time for the things they consider important. Don't be reluctant to raise the issue if you sense your mentor is not prepared or responsible. Do it respectfully and constructively by first recognizing that he or she is busy and that you appreciate the time your mentor is spending with you. I've had to go as far as asking mentors if their interests have waned, and, if so, saying perhaps it would be best for us both to find other alternatives. That has been far more the exception than the rule, but it may come down to your having to address this issue. However, don't be the one who is unprepared or acting disinterested—*ever.*

Doing the Right Thing

The last point to keep in mind relates to one of my favorite sayings: always do the right thing. Supporting your mentor openly can be highly effective in demonstrating your appreciation for their time and effort. One positive action is speaking highly about your mentor; in doing so you are building the mentor's résumé as a credible asset in your development. Remember while you're doing this never to compromise your agreements about how to treat the confidentiality of what takes place and what has been said and shared between mentor and mentee.

As a matter of fact, one of the very first things I did as a mentor in establishing our rules of engagement was to initiate dialogue with a proposed mentee on our confidentiality boundary conditions. Did we want to dictate that what we said between us stayed only between us? Did we want to leave it open to the discretion of both parties? Or did we want to take an approach that removed any and all limitations on sharing information with others? There is obviously no one right or wrong answer that would fit all situations. Again, my unwavering guidance to you is to work with your mentor during your initial conversation to establish your confidentiality boundary conditions, and then do all you can to respect them.

Before we get into a greater level of specificity on how to prepare for conversing with your mentor, I want to share with you a personal story. Aside from the driveway dialogue with my father that helped energize me to become something more, this next story is one that I will always point to as also having a most significant impact on my professional development. It too demonstrates the power of a mentor.

The story dates back to a phase in my life when I had no career aspirations. I had completed a two-year degree at a local community college and had served in the US Air Force. I was employed as an engineering laboratory technician for a large global conglomerate's energy division. I worked with degreed engineers on metallic alloy development and testing.

At the time I thought I was professionally challenged. I was enjoying my work, but as I look back, I'm not sure I was making any real difference. Yes, I had a job to do and I did it well. But aside from that, I can't define an instance where doing that also resulted in my doing something special or unique that couldn't have been done by someone else. I didn't recognize that making a difference was important or possible. I was compensated well for the effort I put forth. The engineers I worked with, my peer technicians, other team associates, and my supervisors cited my performance as exemplary throughout my tenure in that role. On the surface I was happy. I was not in any way familiar with what a mentor really was, and I was not under the formal direct guidance of anyone relative to my career or personal development. At the time, that was not important to me. Perhaps I am describing your current situation.

Then something completely unexpected occurred. My direct supervisor called me into his office. That had not been arranged in advance. The only other times I had been in his office were to talk about specific work assignments and to have my annual performance review. I'm sure you can imagine what was going through my mind at the time. Had I done anything wrong? Not that I could recall. He had never called me into his office before, so I thought I was going to be let go due to the rumored budget challenges. So many things were going through my mind because I had not experienced that from him. His method of communicating with all of his staff was infrequent and usually focused on a specific task, so I did not expect an impromptu dialogue. Needless to say, I was quite anxious.

When he closed the door behind me, we both sat down. He started by telling me how much he appreciated the quality and the quantity of my efforts and was sorry he was not in a position to compensate me for my true worth to the company. His reasoning was valid. The company, like many others, had policies on job titles, roles and responsibilities, experience levels, and compensation that all tied back to educational and tenure variables. He went on to tell me he knew the nature of my work was similar to a degreed engineer's, and there was a two-to-one differential in my salary compared to that of an engineer with equitable tenure. That was not news to me. He continued to tell me that because of the corporation's policy, he was not in a position to offer me either a substantial change in compensation or a promotion to an engineering job.

But at that point in my career, those things were not important to me. You see, I was unknowingly accepting my own mediocrity. Equally troubling, as I would soon find out, was that I did not see the potential in myself that others saw in me.

Then the supervisor surprised me. He said something like this: "Bob...I am going to offer you some advice, for what it's worth and if you're willing to listen."

I hesitated, feeling anxious, and then responded, "Sure."

He continued, "I think you have an unlimited professional future in front of you. I'm going to tell you that if you stay on your present course, you will most likely fall woefully short of your true potential. If I were you, I would go home tonight and think about leaving the company. Get yourself focused on getting your engineering degree starting this fall, graduate, and come back here and aspire to run this organization!"

Whoa! Are you kidding me? I paused for a moment and thought to myself. I was stunned, shocked, confused, and afraid. I was already in the process of creating all the reasons why, at that point in my life, that was not possible. My divorced mom was somewhat dependent on me for assisting her financially. How would I pay for college? Could I even find a credible school to accept me? I was imagining life in a college dorm at the age of twenty-four. I hadn't studied formally in more than four years. My high school education and community college experience and performance had not been earth-shattering. The list of excuses grew the longer I spent time thinking about it.

As we made idle chitchat, I started thinking about what he had told me and how huge that step must have been for him to take. How unselfish of him! He was willing to deal with replacing me and the effort to transition all my work to another technician for the benefit of encouraging me to do something more with my life. He not only showed his concern for my likely long-term underachievement, but he also wanted to play a role in helping me actually do something about it. He wanted me to take control of my development. That was something that had not really crossed my mind up to that point in my life.

I worked the rest of the day the best I could, and then went home to think about what had happened. I did not truly understand the magnitude of it all. That was yet another instance, like the one in the driveway with my father, when my life changed in a way that would set the foundation for the personal growth and professional achievements that were in store for me—all of which, at the time, I had not yet even imagined were possible.

While I will spare you all the details of what transpired next, I listened to what he told me to do but took it a step further. I took even more control of my life that day and have never really let go since. While I surely went through periods where it took on a lesser degree of importance, I held on to two very important things: if something special were going to happen for me, I was the one who had to make that happen, and the value of having mentors in my life was immeasurable.

I learned several other things after I reflected on that discussion. Even now I think about it daily, and I gain additional perspectives that I apply. Again, how unselfish of him—he was truly interested in my development even at the cost to him and his organization's short-term effectiveness. Later on I recognized the slight chaos his unselfish act created was temporary and would offer someone else the opportunity to excel as my replacement. I never forgot that last point. Every time I had the chance to encourage any employee of mine to take advantage of a development opportunity, I reflected on the important role I played, the encouragement I offered the employee, and the opportunity the situation would present to another employee looking for a new and exciting challenge.

It took me some time to understand that a minor disruption in my organization due to an employee's taking advantage of an opportunity to excel was actually not a disruption at all. It was there that I truly began to understand my place as a leader and a mentor. That experience helped me to appreciate the importance of career-success planning. It made me so much more than I ever thought I could be at the time.

My first true mentor passed away from cancer while I was a student in engineering school, so he was not alive to see what he had helped me accomplish. However, I am quite sure he is both pleased and proud of how effective he was in changing my life forever. I will never forget him, what he did for me, and how instrumental his actions were in shaping my life's journey. There is not a single day that goes by in which I don't think about him and his impact. I vowed to always try to give back in some way just as he had given to me.

Let's look at this from the opposite angle—one that is perhaps more common in the workplace. What happens if one acts more selfishly and puts his or her personal interests far in front of what may be better in the aggregate? There are the obvious issues of stagnation, loss of passion and energy to do what it takes, hard feelings from the lack of developmental support, and perhaps even a degradation of the quality of output from an organization that operates with this all going on. But some even more disturbing things can happen without our realizing it at the time.

I had been in a project management role for fewer than ten years. My primary financial team member was an outstanding employee in every aspect. He was highly competent, dedicated, very social, collaborative, and driven by results. His word was his commitment. He was also a very close friend; in fact, he was my closest friend. We spent a lot of time together as our families grew and the lines across work, friends, and family blurred.

I'm not sure why I didn't really notice the early signs, but I will remember that day for the rest of my life. He came into my office visibly emotional. He tried to explain to me the impact all the work-related travel and stress had on his balancing work and life. I knew what was coming, so I shut down and stopped truly listening. I heard him tell me he was leaving the company to pursue other interests in line with a more balanced lifestyle, which was important to him and his family. My reaction? Shock, upset, uncaring, selfish, and argumentative summarize it well. I know it surprised him due to the nature of our friendship and family history, but it was how I reacted.

His last two weeks at work were very tense as we tried to work through the transition of his responsibilities. He was so excited to begin his new challenge, but I did not share his enthusiasm. The entire dynamic had a dramatic impact on our friendship, which took a turn for the worse. Once we stopped communicating, our families reacted in kind, and we did not communicate for eight years. Yes, you read that correctly. And it was all my doing, every single bit of it, and it all could have been avoided had I handled it quite differently. It could have been such a rewarding experience for everyone, but at the time, that potential outcome never even crossed my mind.

My narrow views and acts of selfishness took away the tremendous opportunity to enjoy the sort of true friendship that does not come around very often. All of that happened because he wanted something more, something different, and to take advantage of an opportunity that would provide him a much better balance in his life. What's more important than that? To him, at the time, nothing was. However, my ego and the professional disruption his decision caused took precedence, and the impact was far more significant than I'd ever imagined it could be.

The ramifications of your actions and the actions of others can have tremendous and lasting impact in both positive and not-so-positive ways. If you recognize and practice the important role you play in helping others unconditionally become all they can be, you will be able to avoid the situation in which I put myself.

It took me eight years to grow up. A day did not go by when I didn't think about it. My pride, embarrassment, and ego all got in the way until I reached a point where I could reach out and mend the broken friendship. I called him up, and, after getting past the initial and expected mutual expressions of positive emotions, we began the reconciliation process. Since then our friendship has blossomed, and our families have reunited. We now have a business relationship where he has become my most trusted financial adviser. In retrospect, what a mistake I made! It was all on me. But, as with everything, I ask you not to look back and ask why, but instead to learn from your mistakes and look forward to the next opportunity to do it the right way.

At this point you should have gathered enough data to begin the next phase of the process of selecting your mentor. I always created an initial order of priority by listing the individuals I felt would be the best mentors. I would eliminate from my list anyone who fell short in areas I felt were important and/or who didn't make the cut as I assessed their mentorship qualities. Remember, many of your assumptions may not be totally

> *Learn from your mistakes, and apply what you've learned at every opportunity— without exception.*

accurate simply due to your unfamiliarity with all or some of the individuals under consideration. This is completely natural and an expected outcome. Don't allow this phase to have a life of its own. It's time to move on.

Now, you need to get ready to reach out to your candidates and request a dialogue with each that should last no more than fifteen to thirty minutes. This will be adequate time to determine their levels of interest and to validate quickly the findings you've gathered on the various individuals as you prepared for this step. Before you actually reach out, I strongly suggest you prepare your approach.

You will need to be aware of any individual's or organization's operating style. Is it normal practice to approach the individual directly? This is the way I preferred to operate. I worked very hard to accommodate anyone who wished to speak with me, and to be as flexible as I could to allow interchanges to occur. Word of my approachability and accessibility spread fast, so be aware of this. Not everyone is like that; some are far more formal. Don't let that deter you!

Whether it works out for you to contact this individual directly or if you feel it best to work with someone else to arrange the dialogue, you must be prepared. Let's say, for example, you have five skills you feel are important for you in a mentor. Before you make any final decisions on who you will select, try to align subject matter experts with your skill needs. Who better to learn from than those who understand the skills and practice them impeccably?

Take the easiest approach to engaging your prospective mentor. It may take some time to connect; give that person a chance. I always considered it an honor when people asked me to be their mentor, and I can assure you I'm not alone in feeling that way. Here's what I suggest you do as you prepare to reach out and as you engage:

- ⇒ Prepare a short biography of yourself that includes things such as a summary of who you are, a bit about your values, your interests, what's important to you and where you see yourself going in the short-, mid- and long-term. Anything goes here as it's just to give the prospective mentor an indication of who you are and what you are about.

- ⇒ Explain that you are taking an active role in your development and why. You need to say all of this with conviction so your commitment can be felt through your words!

- ⇒ Explain that you understand the characteristics and value of a mentor-mentee relationship and are in the process of seeking a mentor. Explain your expectations and what you plan to contribute to the process.

- ➲ Be sure you indicate that you do not have any ulterior motives and that you are not looking for anything other than some insights into what it takes to become successful.

- ➲ Take some time in between each of these steps to allow the individual to engage, ask questions, and ask for further clarification.

- ➲ While this is all occurring, it is vital that you are assessing the individual's level of interest or engagement. This takes some practice and is more natural for some than for others. But over time you will have enough experience and insight to gauge this rather accurately. Don't spend time if the interest is not mutual.

If you strongly sense little to no interest or energy, politely thank the individual for his or her time and perspective; perhaps go so far as to write a personal thank-you note, but then move on to the next person. You can simply say you appreciate the person spending some time with you and that you understand that the demands on his or her time at that point may not support your engaging in a mentor-mentee relationship. Perhaps you can suggest leaving any follow-up for a time that would be more acceptable. Or you can create a similar message on your own, based on what you thought you experienced. I have found that some potential mentors like to take time to think it over, perhaps asking others about you first. Everyone likes to be around winners and people with potential.

Don't be discouraged if you get some responses indicating a lack of interest. Take the high road and move on. It could be a time constraint on the part of that person and more than likely may have nothing to do with you personally. I have sent thank-you notes to individuals who then reached back out to encourage follow-up sessions to continue our conversations. If all else feels good, accept the invitation to have an additional discussion.

As you work your way through the entire list of candidates, I am hopeful you will find two or three individuals who express enough interest to proceed. The number is not magic here. There is a chance you will have to add additional names to assess before you find those select few. But again, this is not a science; it's more of an art, and the path to the end result will vary— sometimes greatly—due to individual style, personal situation, level of formality, and geographical location, to name a few possibilities. Be patient, stay the course, remain focused and solid in your convictions. It will be worth the effort.

Let's assume you now have a list of two or three individuals who on first pass appear to be interested in moving forward. Now for some additional preparation! There is a lot of work involved when taking the lead in your development. I am sure you now have a better understanding of why so many people don't have a real interest in taking on such a responsibility. As I said earlier, because this process requires a true commitment, some choose to take the easy way out and simply look to blame someone else for their own lack of action and success. Don't fall victim to this; remember, nothing in your development is going to become a reality without you taking charge! No excuses, no exceptions.

What do you need to prepare now? Initially seek insight into your plan with your potential mentor. Collaborative actions such as this will not only help your plan evolve into a better product, but potentially create some ownership on the part of your proposed mentor.

Next, refer back to the list you created. Take another good, hard look at the skills, values, and attributes you possess as well as those areas where perhaps further exposure is needed. One of the things you're going to want to gain insight into in this initial session are the skills your mentor feels are or were—and continue to be—instrumental in his or her success. Don't be shy here, and be fully prepared. Practice active listening. Take copious notes, and if something remains unclear, ask for further clarification.

Anything is fair game. Aside from the more tangible hard skill sets, hopefully your potential mentor will raise other subjects, such as interpersonal skill development. We will talk much more about this later on. Discussions may even become a bit more tactical. You may talk about the increased stress levels that come with the additional exposure and visibility you will receive as you progress. You may hear more about the need to sacrifice a bit of your balance between work and life given the demands of a particular role. Have the skill list you originally created at hand because you will likely need to modify it as a result of these conversations. The bottom line is to have no predetermined limitations, boundaries, or conclusions on any aspect of this step until you've had a chance to absorb all the input.

Now you must focus the dialogue on the specific things about which you want to know more. Be mindful of your top priorities and your need to manage the time you will have with each mentor candidate. Your skills list may include other things like expectations, important networking opportunities, time management, and balance between time spent on work-related issues versus life's other demands. Consider any information you can gather at this point in the process as important.

Finally, you need to think about what you expect to accomplish during the time you have allocated for this initial conversation. I suggest you openly share this with your candidate. Place your most important elements upfront to ensure they receive adequate coverage. Do not be concerned if you run out of time. If things progress, and it is your intention to continue with the relationship, you will find ample reasons to meet again soon, and you will be prepared for that follow-up session.

I can tell you from my vast set of experiences that if the connection is strong, you will feel like there is never enough time. It passes quickly, but the energy level can be quite high. This is exactly what you want. Focus on the right things with a high degree of energy. Great things are bound to result!

You have placed yourself in a position to meet with each individual you feel offers the best opportunity for you to gain the most perspective and who have expressed an interest in getting to know you. Let the introduction and familiarization process play out, and use the insights you gain throughout this process as additional information with which to make an informed decision. Now you can proceed to set up your initial session prepared with a plan you will share with your mentor.

Focus on the challenges that are significant and matter most.

Engaging in active listening is as crucial now as it's ever going to be. Remember, time is a valuable commodity, and if you're truly as good as you lead others to believe you are, spending your time on efforts that add value is very important. The same holds true for your mentor. I've never run into anyone I considered a winner who had a tremendous amount of time to waste. Your shared role here is to ensure that, under any circumstances, you both are going to spend time on all the important things and not engage in a lot of frivolous dialogue that brings little to no value to the process.

Don't be defensive when you hear things you may not want to hear or can't appreciate at the time. As a mentor, once it became apparent a mentee had no regard for what I was offering or became defensive when I told him or her some additional things to work on, my interest and enthusiasm levels waned.

An employee who had just graduated and started his employment with me stopped by my office one evening unplanned for a bit of informal career development dialogue. He started off by asking me what he needed to do to get my job. That was an admirable question, but initially his true intentions were unclear. As I began to go through my journey with him, sharing the things I had needed to do along the way, his eyes glazed over. When I got into a discussion of the balance of work and life, I lost him completely. The only thing I could conclude was that he had a desire, but he wasn't willing to do what it would take. I lost any remaining enthusiasm I had for the dialogue, and he left the office, never to be seen again. He left the company as well, and perhaps we were all better off. Sometimes it simply doesn't work out.

I also do not appreciate a lack of preparation in advance; this leads me to believe that mentees are unwilling and/or unable to commit themselves to the tasks at hand. If that ends up being the case, I usually bow out—but not until I have offered direct feedback as to my reasoning. Some people go away and never return, but many others ask to come back. When they do, they are better prepared.

Take note of your time; try to find the right way to get the conversation to wind down so you can finish promptly. I do not appreciate it when a mentee incorrectly assumes our dialogue can or will continue beyond our appointed time slot. If I am OK with extending the session for a while longer, I will state that; if it works for the mentee then all is fine. But be ready to wrap up the discussion and to leave on time.

However, don't leave before committing to taking your mentor's guidance into consideration. Consolidate it with other input you've received and your own views. Furthermore, commit to getting back to your mentor with your views on the next steps, and, if it is your mutual desire to do so, plan a follow-up dialogue in the near-term to share your thoughts and plans for action. End the session with a firm handshake, good eye contact, and a warm and sincere thank you. As you walk away and your head is spinning, take a moment to be thankful for what has just occurred, and be proud of the steps you have taken thus far. Remember, this relationship is a two-way street. You will both learn from each other, and do all you can to make both of you proud of what you have and what you plan to accomplish down the road.

To close out this chapter, I want to remind you that this entire mentor-mentee dynamic is nothing more than gaining insight through subject matter experts or those who possess skills that you need. You will likely not learn everything from this one set of individuals, but you will know what you must focus on next. That is the key!

CHAPTER 5

THE WILL TO PREPARE

After you have had the opportunity to meet with your mentors, your head will likely be spinning from all the dialogue and feedback you received up to that point. Remember the purpose here. It was not to sit down and take notice of all your positive accomplishments to date; the process all along called for you to focus on your skills inventory, with an emphasis on the skills those experts felt were necessary to execute the responsibilities of a role to which you aspire.

There is a lot of work to do, but as with anything, effort applied is proportional to outcome received. So now is the time to recharge yourself and start the process of mapping out the next steps of your plan. I found it helpful to step away from the details for a short time to let the sessions' impact settle a bit before I started to develop my road map. This amount of time varies by individual and will reflect whatever else is going on in your life. I find in retrospect that it was like writing this book: some days the words and thoughts are flowing well, yet on other days it's a struggle to collect my thoughts and document them in a cohesive manner. So what I suggest to you is to maintain your purpose of making forward progress, and in parallel pick a time to work on further developing your plan when you can be totally focused.

When the time comes to create your road map using everything you've learned up to this point, where do you begin? While you certainly can use one of several online career development tools, I found many of them restricted my thinking by being too specific. Conversely, sometimes they were so general and obvious in nature, the utility I would gain from them would be marginal. I felt it would be most helpful for me to formulate my plan my way. I created my own templates and formats and learned as I went along.

I will share with you now the major elements of my personal planning content and offer my perspective of the utility of each part of it. I will say once again that this is not a science, and there is no right or wrong approach here; incorporating an online tool or using another tool that is available to you may very well work. You can choose to duplicate a plan structure similar to the one I will describe for you or something entirely unique that you prefer to create on your own. The obvious and most important thing here is that you develop and utilize a plan that will be useful to you.

In some cases you have thoroughly laid the groundwork through the skills and values assessment process documented in chapter one. In some cases the groundwork has just commenced or has not yet begun, so the objective is to take advantage of everything you have learned up to this point and build the substance around the pieces requiring more effort.

Setting goals without a plan for their accomplishment defines failure.

For me the first section of a plan always focuses on the detailed inventory of my skills, values, and defining traits and a summary of both my personal and professional interests. That's why we create the inventory in the first place.

Second, it is time for you to think more about what your next professional challenges will be in both the short-term and the long-term. It is also the time for you to reflect back on all the dialogues you have had with your prospective mentors. Draw from their personal experiences, recommendations, successes, and setbacks. I am asking you to do this now not so you will mimic or attempt to duplicate their paths, but so you can use the wealth of information you have gained and combine it with the outcome of any other research you may have done to create your own unique way forward. This part of the planning process will not be as well refined and will likely be far more subjective than the skills assessment exercise as there is an obvious and purposeful lack of clarity here. This is both natural and expected. You are supposed to be thinking about your longer-term objective, thus less definition is to be expected. I also suggest you take an ample amount of time to think this through as thoroughly and carefully as you know how. You will have to make some very important choices as a result of the outcomes of this part of the process, so the quality of your efforts here is crucial.

Third, make a thoughtful attempt at examining all the information you have gathered relative to your skills, knowledge, values, and experience needs, and begin to place a priority on the attainment of each. Apply some of your intuition and perspective to decide which of these you should tackle first. Ask yourself if any of these skills are complementary or related. Focus on developing multiple skill sets in parallel.

I recognize that the composition of your specific needs will vary widely based on where you are in your professional journey. But regardless of whether you're a more seasoned professional or less mature in your professional development, for example, and you feel team building and conflict resolution are two skill sets to which you need additional exposure, you can quickly envision the similarities between the two processes and seek the direct counsel of others to gain access to these skill sets. You can even take it one step further and begin to apply some of them as you carry out your daily tasks when working collaboratively and/or dealing with some level of conflict within a team. This provides you the unique opportunity to gain access to the basic skills outlined by your mentor, other subject matter experts, and your peers.

Combine those insights with information gained from personal research and perhaps some additional seminar or coursework to begin applying them in a real-world setting. It might be helpful to attend courses or seminars or to pursue some level of training to gain exposure to certain skill sets. I can clearly and without hesitation state that there is no substitute for applying these principles on the job or on an assignment that involves other individuals. Without the opportunity to put these principles into practice, the chances of your converting the skill needs into skill strengths in the time frame necessary to make a real difference will be greatly challenged. Going to a class or reading articles about dealing with something as complex and important as conflict resolution can be very instructional. Reading about how to ask the right questions, how to listen carefully to responses, and how to apply your experience and intuition to portray circumstances accurately may also be useful. Material on how to draw on those experiences to develop solutions that are reasonable, fair, effective, and instructive while allowing the parties involved to continue with their responsibilities and put the experience behind them is easy reading—believe me!

Now, take that same situation and apply it in a real-world setting. The people involved are in a heightened state of anxiety, and it's likely they're not thinking clearly or even rationally at some stage during the process. Their personal biases come into play, and there you are, trying to help these individuals grow as they learn from and move beyond this conflict. You can't just close the book and hope the problem goes away on its own. This is real life.

Whether you are thinking about what you want to do, are seeking your first role, or are a seasoned professional, gaining exposure to actual circumstances will draw on skill sets you may or may not yet possess. As I have noted, learning through experience is a most effective way to grow. The purpose of this is to gain skill set access and credibility. Take charge, get these skills sets prioritized, seek out those who have the expertise, and move forward toward applying and learning.

In this specific case, for example, find someone who is known as a person who deals well with conflict for some guidance. This, as well as reading and learning from the experiences of others, will form a foundation of knowledge. But after that is all said and done, it's best to put yourself in a position to experience the challenges in real life. Please know that it does not matter if you are still preparing for your first professional challenge, if you are already a part of a corporate organization, or if you are running your own single-employee business; you will deal with this part of your development in the same way in any situation. Remember, the quality of your preparation will always shape the quality of the end result.

Let's suppose a subset of these skill set needs or attributes falls into the category of things you don't particularly enjoy doing. You have given this a lot of thought already as you included them in the skills assessment exercise we discussed in chapter one. This happens more than you can imagine. My feeling is that, like it or not, we all have to spend time doing things at work or in other aspects of our daily lives that directly conflict with the other things we would much rather do. For this specific and real-life situation, I offer you the following: accept the fact that every role contains tasks you may not enjoy doing. Don't use the discomfort associated with this as an excuse to avoid them or not do them at all. That's what others may choose to do, but not you! Winners use aversion to fuel their passion to practice lifelong learning. Try hard to convert this shortcoming and dislike into a skill set strength. If you want to grow and gain an immediate and gratifying sense of accomplishment, tackle head on something you have always tried to avoid, and master it. Convert it to something people will identify as a skill set strength of yours. The sense of accomplishment will be unparalleled, believe me.

It used to be that just the idea of speaking in front of even a handful of people was enough to make me physically ill. I avoided it at all costs. I also took courses on how to make more effective presentations. But in the absence of practicing the new skills I was exposed to, I saw very little improvement in my comfort level.

While I didn't truly recognize it at the time, I would soon be exposed to an experience with a fellow student that would demonstrate directly for me the power of learning how I might be able to tackle my fears through understanding other people's challenges. At that time a work associate and I were both pursuing MBAs. The associate looked like a model student on the surface, but he seemed always to fall short on test scores. What I discovered was that in the process of his preparing for exams and trying to balance a personal life, a full-time job, business travel, and evening classes, he took shortcuts. By doing things such as not focusing more on the aspects of the topics he didn't understand well, he became complacent and comfortable by placing his emphasis on the less challenging issues and exercises. That clearly led to his going into testing situations less than adequately prepared. Even more of an issue was that he *knew* he was going into the tests unprepared.

That turned out to be a major source of anxiety when he took exams. What could I learn from his experience? I began to examine the anxiety that accompanied my attempts at public speaking. While the situations were quite different, the causes, as I learned, were identical. It became clear that I was spending far too much of my limited time and energy worrying about the questions people might ask me or how they would perceive me. Instead of applying that anxiety and energy into fully preparing for my talk, I became more anxious and thought far too much.

Over time I learned how to improve my focus, prepare more completely, and anticipate better the needs of the audience. That manifested in a strong form of confidence, energy, and passion that continues to serve me well to this day. I became used to speaking to groups regardless of the number. It became unimportant whether my audience was a single individual or thousands at a commencement address. What mattered was that I was fully prepared. So, face your fears with conviction and use the opportunity to convert a skill set shortcoming into a strength. Learn from the experiences of others as I did from my MBA classmate. There is nothing quite like the things we are exposed to in our daily lives to help us learn and improve each and every day.

Now let's talk about the roles your supervisors or other people in your circle of influence play in your skill attainment planning. If your attitude is positive, if you remain committed to owning the process, you must then work toward helping

> *Face your fears head on and become more complete.*

all those around you understand what you are doing, why you are doing it, and what you expect from them in the process.

What do you expect from your supervisors or other influential people in your life? It seems like an easy enough question on the surface. There are no answers that are totally correct. Each individual is different, and the approach and role each thinks he or she should play in the development of the members of the team varies widely. Make sure to share the details of the plan with everyone and do all you can to create additional opportunities to support the specifics of the plan with those around you. Both of these approaches are very effective. Take the time to go through the personal commitment you made to yourself and make it clear you have taken the responsibility to outline the development plan for your professional life. Go into the specific learning and findings relative to your skill set assessments and offer insights you've gained from your mentors. Furthermore, let others understand how you currently see your short-term, midterm, and long-term career objectives and that it is your full intent to focus and work tirelessly toward them.

All the while you are, albeit indirectly, helping these individuals understand how important this entire process is to you. Supervisors who are not actively involved in the career planning processes of the members of their team are not rare. You need to be prepared even if you are not asked to offer up what role your supervisors play in all of your planning. This is where you have to be direct, constructive, polite, and persistent all at the same time. Be prepared to offer the fact that you expect their understanding and would appreciate their full support. It is all about reaching your full potential, learning, having fun, and making a difference each and every day.

I should tell you that many supervisors I have had throughout my professional career were committed to keeping me busy and compensating me fairly while offering a variety of tasks and assignments that were important to them. The concept of matching assignments with skill sets and attributes that require further development is not a common practice. I would not call it selfish by any means. I would say the thought of keeping me right where I was offered them both comfort and organizational stability. But this simply was not acceptable to me, and I imagine your situation is not going to be much different. Taking charge is important—critically important. Whether we work for someone else now or will in the future or we own businesses, we all have bosses. You owe it to your supervisors and your customers to be all you can be. It's about being your best at what your life's calling is. Mediocrity is not an option.

You need to accomplish all this development focus without compromising your responsibilities at your current job or your studies. In my view, support means enabling, not impeding, your process of finding activities that further skill set development. It also means you and those helping you are creating an environment that is conducive to your progression. Support means

> *It's all about being your best.*

looking for opportunities that will both challenge you to leave your comfort zone and offer you opportunities to expand your network and gain additional visibility. What you really want is for your supervisors and others in your circle of influence to want only the very best for you. If that's currently the case, you are fortunate. If it's not the case, the time has come to do something about it.

After I successfully made the transition from individual contributing engineer to program manager, I was responsible for leading a project from concept, design, and manufacturing through marketing, sales, and after-sales support. The contract was with an international government organization. The product design was complete, and we were in the initial phases of delivering the product to our launch customer and other markets. My presence and involvement at that time was crucial.

While that was going on, a very unique opportunity came up involving my potential participation in a corporate-sponsored leadership development program. In it I would, over a two-year period, be exposed to a number of diverse assignments and experiences that aligned quite well with my development plan needs. It would have been really easy for my supervisor to deny me that opportunity given the critical stage we were at with our international project. But he did exactly the right thing: he fully encouraged and supported my participation in the program. In return I did all I could to ensure seamless leadership transition on the project I'd been heading. Ownership, a plan, personal drive, exposure, and a very unselfish leader all came together to provide me with a tremendous opportunity to develop my skills further. The same can happen to you!

> *Everyone in your circle of influence should want only the best for you.*

At this point in time, you have developed:

- ⇒ Your current perspectives on your short-term, mid-term, and long-term career aspirations.

- ⇒ Your inventory of skill set needs that support the achievement of your aspirations.

- ⇒ The roles you and others play in implementing your plan.

You now have a clear definition of the types of skills in which you need additional exposure, a definition of your role, and an outline of your supervisors' roles. Now it's time to map out the specifics relative to the actions required.

Again referring to the template introduced in chapter one, it's important for you to define for each skill and/or attribute a set of specific dates by which you expect to achieve some level of expertise. I suggest you try to balance being aggressive with realism. The period you choose should serve as motivation and not be so unrealistic that it seems pointless. The time frame in the big picture should coincide with and perhaps support a date when you may need to be ready to take on your next role. Use your short-term, midterm, and long-term career objectives and dates as milestones that your skill set development dates must support. Be committed to these dates, and think long and hard before you acquiesce to moving any of them further out once they're established.

Now that you have some specific dates, you must think deeply about getting exposure to the skills you need in a way that supports developing them into expertise. There is no magic here; it's all about planning the basics. Find out which roles, assignments, tasks, and special projects could likely yield the exposure you need. Don't be shy. Get out and actively learn about such opportunities. Seek them out! This will drive the refinement of your action plan.

Spend your time focusing on what you can control and understand the things you cannot.

I have mentioned this before, but it bears repeating: gaining exposure to these skills in a job shadowing, real-world experience has tremendous merit. Simple introductions to the concepts are effective for gaining basic skill competencies, but there is nothing like the real thing to give one the best learning perspective. Planning to gain access to these skill needs is important; actually defining how you'll go about getting the opportunities to learn them will take a tremendous amount of work and creativity.

The primary and most obvious challenge is that in most cases, you have very little control over how this job shadowing experience will specifically turn out in advance of actually engaging in the exercise. Yet at the same time, you are accountable for your plan and your development. So you need to take the lead on developing the plan through which you will gain this exposure. Pursue opportunities to job shadow in organizations in which the chances of gaining exposure to certain skills are high. For example, if you're looking to gain exposure to such skills as conflict resolution, employee performance evaluations, and team building, spend time job shadowing in your organization's human resources department.

Of course you will need to work out the logistics with your supervisor and human resources first. You will also need to ensure you don't compromise your obligations to your current assignment. The quickest way to impede your supervisors' support of your development is to impact your performance on your current job negatively, not to mention what this will say to others about you and what's more important to you. No matter what degree of importance you assign to taking responsibility for your development, it should not be at the expense of your fulfilling commitments you've already made to others.

If you're not at that point in your development yet, let's say you're still a student, the same exact concept applies. You still have other primary obligations to your schoolwork, and while seeking out internships and other job shadowing experiences in parallel with your classroom activities is important, it can't be at the expense of serving your primary purpose as a student first and foremost! You may have to make a choice, and it's a choice only you can make and one you must make.

I can remember several situations in which I was job shadowing to get exposure to specific sets of skills. I recall it was usually a difficult challenge to balance my time and energy to ensure I did everything with the appropriate levels of respect and focus. It was also most important that I did not compromise the quality of my work. You may have a similar experience. You will also likely encounter different quality levels, particularly in job shadowing assignments. I've seen this happen with college student interns working at a company for short periods of time as well as with more seasoned employees looking for skill exposure and enrichment while on the job. It's human nature for people not to put as much energy or passion into your job shadowing experience as you might like or expect, so choose these experiences wisely. So, what can you do to help you make the best choice possible?

Again, use your network to find out all you can in advance of making any commitments. If you detect a reluctance to participate, move on to seek a new, more effective experience. I also suggest you work hard when planning any experience to create a set of assignment expectations that all involved can agree on so everything is clear and well understood beforehand. If the experience falls short of your expectations, try to communicate that before frustration sets in. Perhaps the assignments are not challenging enough, and your host is reluctant to give you meaningful tasks; if that is the case, speak up! Tell him or her that you want more challenges. Don't just go through the motions, and don't just write it off as a bad experience. This is your time that's being spent, and you need to treat it as something precious. Speak up if your expectations are not being met. If it still falls short after that, you likely need to move on. But know that seeking out extra assignments and risky, complex roles was instrumental in my development.

Early on in my career, I became known as the guy to lead a proposal development process because I knew how to win. That was not always the case, believe me. It all started with an initial job shadowing role in which the proposal development process was a real skill set need, as I had identified in the plan I had discussed with my mentor. I followed that up with ad hoc assignments through which others sought me specifically to lead as my skill and confidence levels grew. I saw that skill, among others, grow from a shortcoming to a real strength over a relatively short period. I gained the skill by jumping in, making some mistakes, learning, and refining my approach over the long-term. You learn how to win at anything by first losing and doing something meaningful with what you have learned in the process!

The same thing will happen to you. Word travels far, wide, and quickly about a high-potential individual who will do a great job and do what it takes to win and be successful. So aside from simply seeking out and/or accepting ad hoc assignments to gain skill set exposure, get yourself in a position to expand your professional network at the same time. You can do this through joining and participating in any affinity groups your company or community may sponsor, for example. These are simply individuals, organized to varying degrees, who share a common background, set of interests, or goal. Participating in these groups allows one to get exposure to areas of interest easily, develop a network, and gain tremendous knowledge in the same experience. I have found these types of learning situations to be highly effective while requiring a manageable amount of my time.

At an earlier time in my career, I found myself wanting and needing additional exposure to other cultures adjacent to expanding my customer relationship management skills. I saw market opportunity in Asia and wanted to expand my knowledge of the varied cultures in that region. I joined a group called Friends of Asia, which was simply an affinity group primarily for employees with Asian backgrounds, though it was open and available to any employee as a means to extend our corporation's diversity focus.

My experience in that group was tremendously rewarding to say the least. I found the members, as well as the many ad hoc participants in the frequent gatherings, to be willing and passionate teachers. The results were reflective of the high-quality exposure I gained in doing this. I learned a great deal about their professional and personal values, social skills, respect for their families and elders, their appreciation for family and friends eating together, and got tremendous insight into how to better understand and deal with their more indirect approach to discussing issues. I gained a tremendous amount from participating in these group settings and have offered here a small sampling of those benefits to demonstrate their effectiveness. The observations and learnings you will have will occur quickly, and you will be surprised at how much you can learn over a short period of time if you give yourself the opportunity to take advantage of the experience. I highly recommend you seek out affinity groups. If your company does not currently offer any, or if you are not part of a corporation, your community may have organizations that could offer you similar exposure, as might college and university communities. I ask that you actively look for these opportunities and take advantage of them.

I never felt spending time on any of this was an issue because I always put my primary job first and never compromised the commitments I made to my team. I always kept my supervisors up to speed on my activities relative to the plan I had shared with them. I had some of my most rewarding learning experiences by volunteering for roles that served my need to gain additional skills.

You may also notice that over time, as people get to know you better, your level of exposure will rise, and because of that, others will seek you out for both incremental assignments and new and exciting longer-term roles. Of the thirteen positions I held throughout my career, the only ones I applied for were my initial job out of college and my very next one six months later. The remaining eleven roles resulted specifically from individuals who sought me out based on what they saw in me and how I might fit the needs of their organizations. You can be in a similar position, but you have to work hard to set yourself apart. And, of course, there are always opportunities to supplement tasks you take on at work with conferences, seminars, short courses, and trainings. I suggest you use these more academic learning opportunities as more supportive rather than primary to your overall learning objectives.

I am always a huge proponent of measuring outcomes to determine achievement. How will you measure success or a specific level of accomplishment? It is vitally important that you push yourself for measurable outcomes to validate to yourself the progress you have made and choose where to focus

> *Set yourself apart by standing above the rest.*

next. It's easy to talk yourself into believing you have made real progress when in fact it was simply a veneer. Be true to yourself. Come up with a set of metrics and measurable outcomes that best apply to your circumstances, and use them to evaluate and validate your progress against your plan.

At this point your plan has evolved to a point where circling back to your mentor, your supervisors, and others in your network will be quite useful to you. Sharing your thoughts with those people serves two purposes: it keeps the lines of communication open, and it underscores the importance you have placed on this entire process and your level of commitment to it. Now that you are beginning to redefine yourself, solicit feedback again from those who have to this point played roles in your development. Recall that learning goes both ways. You may be teaching them to put higher degrees of importance on this process not only for themselves but for others who work for or with them. You are in essence building the characteristics of a leader in taking charge of your development.

As time passes and goals are accomplished, you will need to assess where you are and think about what's next. From there the process continues from a different starting point. Your short-term, midterm, and long-term objectives will likely change.

> *Use progress to fuel your continued focus; never relent.*

Take some time to reflect proudly on the progress you have made to date, and use this to decide what's next with an even greater sense of urgency and energy.

CHAPTER 6

A PICTURE SAYS IT ALL

We are at the point in our journey where we have initiated most of the basic work. We are now going to develop a pictorial view of a general career development plan. I created this step at the very onset of my career development efforts, and it continues to serve me well to this day. The picture provides a total characterization of where I've been and where I currently am, and it provides a direct line of sight to my next objective. It serves as a living document.

This tool has also served to organize my own plan, and I have shared it with those I have mentored and in the classes I teach. It allows me to give them direct insight into how I applied all the principles discussed earlier in this book into a tool that has provided significant utility to me and countless others over time. It is a simple set of techniques that will directly reflect all the effort expended up to this point.

Let's start by getting your mind around the fact that this plan is a written contract with yourself. It is a step-by-step set of objectives and associated actions necessary to achieve any sense of progress. You must treat everything within the plan that has yet to be accomplished as a commitment. You are making a commitment to yourself. You have established actions and timelines for the specific purposes of generating and directing the energy that's necessary for you to have a chance of becoming all you are capable of being. Once you have yourself focused and energized, we are ready to construct the complete plan.

The plan will include the components you have already created and documented using the template provided. Now you will develop your personalized picture of your past, present, and proposed future states.

A commitment to yourself is an obligation to do what you said you would do.

I have created the following image to help you better visualize what we have been talking about thus far. It provides a very clear view of how all these pieces relate to one another and come together as the essential elements of your plan. It will also serve as the basis for creating your personalized career development timeline.

NINE STEPS TO YOUR CAREER DEVELOPMENT PLAN

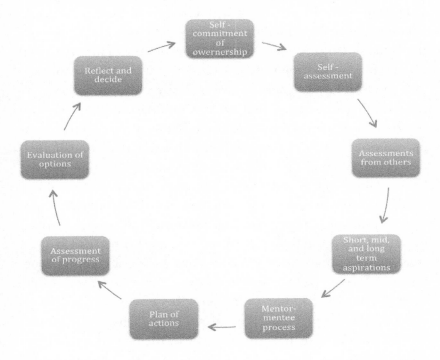

To help guide you through this next important step of the planning process, at the end of this chapter I have included a sample career development plan template and a few simple reminders that will serve as a reference guide for you to use as we go through this discussion. While looking at this sample template, imagine YOUR career development timeline that portrays where you are today and extends to the point in your distant future that is your long-term objective. On my personal timeline I chose to look way out to the time when I thought my formal professional career would end. That may be too far ahead for you to think about, and if so, pick a point in, say, ten years. Think about where you want to be then. If you're a recently graduated lawyer, perhaps becoming a partner in a law firm would be a long-term objective. If you're a public accountant, aspiring to become highly accredited in a specialty field such as tax accounting is in your future, or maybe even becoming a chief financial officer. If you're a student preparing for your first role, I still suggest you think as long-term as you can stretch yourself to visualize choosing something that for you would/could be a natural progression from the initial role you have set your sights on. As an example, if you are an engineering student, perhaps going from that potential first role as a product design engineer to the lead engineer of a product development group may be feasable if that's as far out as you can see. Or, you may think boldly enough to see yourself leading the organizations entire engineering organization as the final role of your career. I can't tell you what that point in time is that streches your personal comfort zone, but what I can do is to again suggest you truly stretch your limits on trying to visualize the future here. Remember, as time passes and your experience inventory grows, the clarity of whats next for you will improve and you will be able to adjust your development accordingly. Regardless of your vocation or where you may be right now in your professional journey, pick something you truly want to achieve. Choose something so very special it will energize you to excel all on it's own.

Lets's put this all together for you now. The next step is to document the conceptual timeline you imagined to achieve that specific objective and look at what it's telling you. If you are bolder than most and are a long-term thinker, try this: as hard as it may seem right now, try to imagine the day when you will retire. Once again, try to imagine your last day of your final role in your professional career. Reflecting back on all that you have accomplished, what you have achieved, and what will define your legacy. Let's add that you are at present a recent college graduate, and you are twenty-two years old. Strictly for instructural purposes, let's suppose your current plan is to work until you are sixty. That would make the end point thirty-eight years from now. I know, it's difficult to think about life in this way at such a young age, but stay with me.

Yes, some of you will want to imagine yourselves and your professional legacies in the year 2052! It's all good; trust me on this. We now have the basics of the picture. It's time to take all that work you have done on inventorying your skills, defining your skill shortages, and reliving all the dialogue you've had with your mentor and others in your network and make it a specific part of this pictorial.

> *The act of looking into the future is not solely for fortune-tellers.*

I want you to focus your attention on where you are right now, with your inventory of strengths and needs on hand. Those needs, you will recall, are based in part on what you need regardless of your vocation of choice. In part, others have offered these insights as attributes you can utilize as you work toward that next career goal. As we have said, you will have put a lot of thought into the feedback and inventory of skills as well as preparing for achieving your next career objective as you get ready to meet with members of your network. The next task is to focus on and create energy around the achievement of your development goals within the time frame you have established to make your next career objective become more of a reality. In doing that, keep a watchful eye on your long-term vision; never lose sight of it! Afterall, that's the endgame here.

As you put the individual pieces of your plan together, you will notice a couple of things begin to take form. You will see the initial phases of the road map for your professional development come to life. Your next goal will be in front of you with your long-term view established, subject to much analysis, scrutiny, questions, debate, and perhaps change over time. Remember this: my very first long-term goal was to be the best individual contributing engineer I could be. Then it changed to program manager, then on to director of programs, vice president and general manager of a business unit, chief operating officer, and finally chief executive officer. I ask you not to worry much about that at this point in the process. Keep it in perspective, but at the same time, keep the tasks at hand in front of you. Focus mostly on what's next and what needs to be done to achieve that objective!

Continuing on, let's say you are coming up on three years at your current job, and you're executing your development plan milestones quite well. You are adding to those important skill set shortages in your inventory. Let's also assume you are beginning to sense a bit less excitement in your current work. I'm not talking about having a routine bad day; what I am saying is you are consistently not as excited as you once were about your current role. You are starting to feel you've made about all the difference you are going to make, and your ability to learn much more in this role is diminishing. This is very common. Every one of us likely has experienced or will experience this to varying extents at some points in our journeys.

I could tell easily when it was happening to me. My enthusiasm to get up in the morning and get into work would wane. The quality of my work suffered, and in general a mild form of malaise set in. Knowing this was simply not me or the way I wanted to spend my time, I saw it as my personal call to action. If this is the situation you find yourself in, and it's not just a temporary concern driven by some unique circumstance, it's time to remember the three most important characteristics a role should offer: learning, having fun, and making a difference each and every day. If you can't find these, you need to begin to look seriously for your next professional challenge. If you choose not to do this, in essence you are signing up to be highly displeased with your professional life. In turn, that inaction will create collateral negative impacts on your personal life and you will be accepting mediocrity all at the same time. As always, that choice is yours!

Assuming that's not the case, the great news is you've been planning for this time and expecting it to come. Because of that, you have thought a lot about this already and have defined your next career role and objective and placed it on your timeline. You know what you want to do, so now it's all about position availability, location, timing, and the competition field full of other potential applicants. While these are the obvious things you might be thinking about in addition to salary and job grade or title, I am going to suggest you expand your perspectives on what is really important. Look at each opportunity while weighing all of these other important things. In addition, look at an organization where you might like to work and its composition of people. Is there a good, diverse staff, or is it more concentrated with experienced people? One is not necessarily better than the other, but organizational composition and dynamics in part define your potential working environment, and you should have a good idea of what you're getting into before you engage. Some people gravitate to roles that play more to their comfort zones while others prefer more challenging environments that will test them daily.

In my case, these more complex opportunities put me in the best positions to learn, make a difference, and enjoy the process all at the same time. You should also pay attention to what peer organizations and leaders feel about your potential new role.

What is the working environment like? What potential opportunities or challenges does that pose for you as a potential new member of the organization?

I suggest one last consideration. The amount of compensation and the job grade or title should be fair and commensurate with the responsibilities that come with the work. However, what I ask you to think about, far more than compensation, is what opportunities this new role will add to your skill set and how it will place you in a position to compete for the next role more successfully. You should also reflect on your long-term, end-of-career professional objective and either revalidate it or redefine it based on what you now feel. As I've stressed many times up to this point, there is no right or wrong here; what you're working on is a statement of objective that is valid at this point in time and is subject to—and *deserves*—constant evaluation and assessment. This also means it's time to reassess the next role for which you will need to prepare. Keep in mind again what the endgame is for you and if it has changed over time. In my case, job title, grade, level, and salary were always secondary; I was confident they would be fair. More important for me were the opportunities to learn, add skills, and develop further toward my full potential.

What needs to occur from now until you reach the ultimate endgame? You must assess your tools and skills continually, work with your mentors and network to determine what skill sets you'll need in order to be highly effective in that next role on your journey. Always be thinking about what's next, but perform your current duties flawlessly.

You will then repeat the process as before: compare the required skills to those you possess and take inventory of your skill shortcomings. Then prioritize your learning objectives and continue on with your development using these areas of focus to direct your energy. Modify your development timeline as time passes and you accomplish goals. Always keep in mind your current state, and, in parallel, think about what's next. This process cycle repeats itself, but now from a different starting point. Remember the real possibility that changes in your career objectives will occur. Keep your timeline document current along with the rest of the supporting information you have created.

Let's look at another possible outcome. You have reexamined your endgame career objective, and you have come to the conclusion that you desire a very different career path from of the one on which you are currently. You've thought about it quite a bit and now feel your long-term objective must change. This happened to me on multiple occasions, and there is a chance it will happen to you too.

As you can imagine, while many skills would be applicable to both your current state and your perceived new future role, there are likely key skill set differences you will require for success. Skills that would likely make an engineer a successfull engineering manager are not all necessarily the same set of skills required should this same engineer aspire to be more focused on the business side of the organization. While there likely may be some common skill needs, these skill differences may in turn require you to modify, and, more likely, bolster your mentor network to include the movers and shakers in the new domain you wish to explore. I am not suggesting you abandon your current mentor roster, but I recommend supplementing your network to include individuals who are better equipped to help get you where you need to go. This is all about expanding your network—an important part of anyone's professional development.

By this point you have created a useful, flexible, and highly functional career development plan. Like every other tool, its effectiveness will be almost totally dependent on how you apply it and your ability to prepare for its implementation. It is a continual process and a plan that will evolve and mature over time. It should always reflect your current state of mind and form the bases of your actions.

I found that my plan served many purposes. Clearly it was my professional road map, with my complete historical and projected career milestones portrayed in a picture for my ready reference. It also included the inventory of all my development accomplishments and my remaining challenges. But much more than that, even at this point in my life, it energizes me when I see where I have been, where I am now, and what may be in store for me in the future. It fuels my desire to become even more than I already am!

I cannot make any specific promises about your particular outcome or level of success. But I can promise that you won't think about how bright your outlook could be until you are not seeing any light at the end of the tunnel. Don't be one of those people who waits for that to occur. I can also promise you that if you practice all I am advocating in this book, accept ownership and accountability for your professional growth, and immerse yourself appropriately in the process, the chances of reaching your full potential will be

> *What you are today is only a waypoint on the journey to become all you can be.*

a lot better. You will begin to believe in the brightness of your future. Stay focused and committed to the process as you face the challenges and opportunities that will surely come your way. Staying power and persistence are key. If you follow my advice, you will be well on your way to achieving the objectives of learning, having fun, and making a difference each and every day.

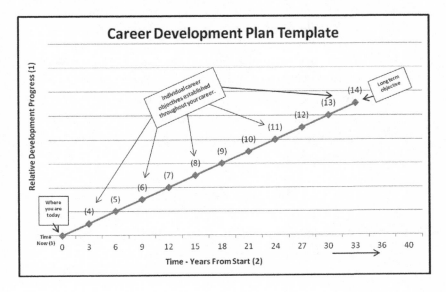

Template Legend

- ⊃ The vertical axis, (1), represents a Relative Level of Development Progress. For this example, we are assuming at Time Now, (3), your current skills inventory is what it is and the focus is on your development towards all future career objectives moving forward, (4) through (14).

- ⊃ The horizontal axis, (2), represents time, in years, from Time Now, (3), to the conclusion of your career where the specific year is to be determined as you develop and evolve your plan.

- ➲ The intersection of the two axes is Time Now, (3), and can either represent the point in time your initial professional role commenced and/or the time that your career development plan was developed.

- ➲ Each successive number, (4) through (14), represents a notional number of individual career objectives spanning from Time Now to your final, long term milestone. Since they are all beyond Time Now, they can only represent your current perspectives on career progression.

Things to Remember

- ➲ Remember that each future career objective is simply a projection based on ones current thinking and situation:

  - These are obviously subject to change over time.

  - These objectives drive your specific skill development focus.

  - It is important you keep your skill development focus aligned with your projected career objectives and the skills necessary to fulfill the requirements of each role.

  - Remember to always strive to find your professional passions and roles that are all well aligned with those passions.

  - Always strive to learn, have fun and make a difference each and every day.

➲ The periods of the time spent in each role, as well as the time spent in between a current role and a projected role, is the time where you:

➤ Work with your mentors, peers, supervisors and others in your network to define and understand what skills are required for any future roles you are considering. Remember to seek out guidance from those individuals who are currently/ have served in those roles you aspire to serve in. It is very impactful to learn from those who know what is required based on their experiences.

➤ Referring to your skills inventory list (template in chapter 1), you will need to add any missing skills to this list, assess your current skill level, define any additional emphasis required, develop an action plan to attain the required skill and competency level along with a timeline to accomplish these actions.

➲ Remember this is a living document and for it to be effective, the process requires your attention and action. Mediocrity is not an option.

CHAPTER 7

SOFTER SKILLS ARE SOMETIMES HARDER

We are at the point where you have the basic understanding necessary to have created a plan that charts a course for your long-term development. Now I want to completely shift your focus from process development to understanding an underserved and underappreciated set of skills as you implement your plan to focus on your professional growth—skills I see as vital to anyone's personal and professional journey, the soft skills. Simply put, these are the skills that relate to people and how to deal with them more effectively.

Soft skills, which several self-proclaimed experts currently credit for the success of many businesses, are just starting to receive the level of attention they deserve and seem commensurate with the heightened advocacy of leadership versus management. It wasn't until later in my professional career that I started to learn about the importance of possessing these skills. I began to study them more and focused hard to make them instrumental parts of my leadership skills base, and the benefits that resulted were both numerous and highly relevant. My company placed a tremendous amount of focus and importance on educating our employess on these skills as the emphasis on leadership development grew rapidly over time. It is for this reason that I am so excited to share my thoughts and experiences on this topic with you now.

My thought here is that if you want to differentiate yourself or your organization, business, or company from others, you must lead, not simply manage. The differences are immense, confusing, and not well understood. I will clarify all this for you throughout this chapter.

Let's begin by differentiating hard skills from soft skills. Hard skills are a specific set of technical skills you can learn through training or attain by reading about them. You can practice them via problem solving or hands-on assignments in a specific industry or profession. Repetiton and memorization are usually the name of the game here. Skills such as software programming, social networking, finance, mathmatics, and accounting are a few examples among thousands of hard skills, which are usually tangible and quantitative, and their levels of expertise are more easily assessed. Once people possess and practice these skills, they can utilize them to manage their performances of daily tasks. Give them jobs for which they possess the necessary hard skills, and they will hopefully go on to do what is necessary to get the tasks completed on time, within budget, and compliant in scope.

Please do *not* misunderstand me here: I am not in any way downplaying the importance of hard skills in any successful business or endeveavor. To the contrary, they are vital! The real issue is that possessing hard skills alone is not nearly enough for an individual or organization to reach its full potential. People who are looking for employment have greater choices for their next development opportunities if they are mobile, adventurous, willing to take chances, and less risk averse. The opportunities could be endless. I feel it's no longer enough simply to offer someone an opportunity to practice a skill. The importance of the working environment, relationships among peers, leader-employee relationships, and the complexity and difficulty of competitive market dynamics are all on the minds of prospective employees. More and more, aspiring individuals want to understand expectations clearly. They want some insight into the direction the organization intends to go and the roles they are going to play within it. Along the way they want to be recognized and compensated in relation to their contributions. Are they going to be able to excel? Increasingly I sense they do not want to be micromanaged, yet they do want to feel they will have the necessary resources and/or access to supervisors if and when they are needed.

This is where soft skills truly come into play. Creating, sustaining, and building an environment such as that described above requires far more than employees who possess only hard skills. Establishing a high-performance work culture is not easy and will always pose significant challenge. Many successful organizations are striving to change their operating styles from being built around title, power, and centralized control to far more open models of vision, change, focus, and direction. These organizations are also most likely driving true employee development at all levels, and, as a result, have much greater opportunities to achieve success because they have placed the importance of people at the top of their priority list. When true leadership is present at every level, individual empowerment will begin to take hold. It will strengthen over time, and, in turn, a deeper appreciation and affinity for the workplace will result. An organization that is empowered, energetic, and passionate about everything in its workplace puts itself in a tremendous position to win.

What are these soft skills? Why are they so important, and can anyone develop them over time? Simply put, soft skills are highly associated with dealing with the human resource—people. They were traditionally thought of as prevalent in more social, less formal environments. The reality is that when we embrace these skills and put them into use, the quality of both our personal and professional relationships becomes much more positive. When you possess and become truly proficient in demonstrating your soft skills, it will be evident in how you carry yourself. It will also impact what people see in you, how you approach all situations, and how you act under all levels of stress. As I've mentioned, these skills are difficult to quantify and are mostly not tangible. Yet the degree of importance they play in the performance of any organization is arguably at the highest levels.

Everyone, regardless of the role he or she plays in any organization, can lead. Leading is *not* reserved for only those who have administrative responsibility over others. It applies directly, and is equally important, to students, individual contributors, small business owners, new hires, and experienced veterans. As for its applicability, how could you expect ever to inspire others to reach their full potential if you don't inspire yourself? Think about it. We've spent the last six chapters talking about taking personal accountability for your development. As I have noted, in order for you to get a feel for your organization and its composition, chemistry, impediments, opportunities, and potential, you first need to understand yourself. Don't shortchange the time and attention necessary to develop your soft skills as you focus on improving your technical skills. Pay equal or possibly more attention to developing your soft skills inventory.

I have, over my professional career, compiled a list of what I believe to be the essential soft skills. While I cannot say I have put these in any order of importance, I can say they are all significant.

Energy

While I can't cite any particular statistics here, I would venture a guess and say that not all highly effective leaders can boast about their academic accomplishments, and maybe they didn't finish very high in their class rankings. I am one of those individuals. My grade school, middle school, and high school performance records would show "just got by" grades. I expended the minimal amount of effort needed to get through school. I went to college after serving in the U.S. Air Force; my mind-set had clearly changed, but my study habits remained as they had been. It took me several semesters to get on track and achieve grade improvements that allowed me to graduate. While I was not at the top of my class, I reached a level that made me proud, which was all that mattered to me. I had tried my very best and did the best I knew how.

So if my grades didn't prove to be instrumental in my achievement, what did? If you were to force me to give you that answer and limit it to two words, I would have to say *personal energy*. I never said "I can't," I always made time for others, I worked hard at not being self-absorbed, and I always put myself in a position to make a difference. The list goes on, but these visible acts were outlets through which my personal energy had a noticeable and greater impact.

Can you name an instance in which you were not inspired when interacting with an energetic individual? I would have a difficult time recalling such an incident from my experiences. The real key to being inspiring versus intimidating is in how you apply your energy and where you direct it and at what time. You can demonstrate energy in a manner that can be intimidating to those with more reserved makeups. Being able to read those around you and understand the topic, the setting, and the purpose both play in the effectiveness of your energy levels.

Exhibiting energy comes naturally to me. It seems I've always possessed high levels of energy. But I can recall several instances when I misdirected my energy. It unwittingly showed up as anger, jealousy, insecurity, or defensiveness when I was simply exerting enthusiasm for the topic. In those cases, I did not achieve the desired impact and realized a less than desirable outcome.

So what if you just naturally don't possess a personality that exudes energy? Perhaps you are more refined and reserved. I have found that anyone, regardless of personality type, can exhibit and demonstrate the energy skill. Perhaps you can try to speak with more conviction and confidence while looking directly in the eyes of those to whom you are speaking. Another tactic I have seen employed is to get involved with efforts and activities in which anxiety levels are high and the pressure to execute is significant. People will notice your involvement, perceive that you care, and be there to offer support. Your actions will emit a sense of energy far more effectively than just the words. This will have a similar effect as offering an inspirational message. Observe those individuals who are known to be energetic, and you will gain a lot of useful insight. Observe them in crowds and see how they engage people.

Another way to exhibit more energy is to focus. Distributing your time and effort by multitasking can, in some circumstances, negatively impact your energy, so do all you can to focus on what's important. This simple act will likely result in an actual sense of accomplishment that is quite energizing in itself. There is a lot to be said about how we can create energy through focusing on and accomplishing one goal or priority at a time. The first step is to understand the importance of energy. Once you do this, focus on finding a way to exhibit more energy in your form and style. To show you truly care and it is not an act, energy must come from within, and you must exhibit it with sincerity.

Passion

This is an intense emotion, a compelling enthusiasm, or desire for something. When I was in the early periods of my professional development, I was naturally drawn to those individuals who exhibited a type of love for what they were doing. I found myself getting energized (energy and passion are complementary) when in the presence of passionate individuals and motivated both directly and indirectly by them. It made me want to emulate that behavior myself because I saw the impact it had on me, and I wanted to impact others in a similar manner. In a way it fueled my desire to better myself and to be in a position to make a difference in others.. It encouraged me to get involved and take advantage of every opportunity to make a difference.

Finding a way to build your passion is all about knowing who you are, thinking about what you want to be, changing the game, looking at challenges as opportunities instead of obstacles, and doing something with those challenges. If you are honest with yourself, you must admit that being around people who are geniunely passionate is exhilarating to you and others. To get exposure to this skill, I again suggest you take every opportunity to get involved with efforts that lend themselves well to applying it. You can volunteer for things you enjoy doing; this allows you to surround yourself with others who have similar passions for a cause. There are unlimited opportunities here. It's up to you to seize them and make the most of them! You can expand your network to include individuals who are passionate about what they do. I find it quite invigorating to see the passion and energy I exhibit having an influence on many others with whom I interact. Once you are aware of the power and influence exhibiting passion has, you will see yourself moving more in that direction over time, just as you will with developing your energy focus. Let me share a story with you now that demonstrates both in action.

I was on an assignment that had me away from home for about eight months. Due to the nature of the assignment, I was simply not able to return home and see my family for an extended period of time. Our team was partnered with another team from Europe, and together our organizations were preparing to offer a complex communications system to the US military. The proposal effort was grueling, filled with tension, deadlines, and demanding customers. We were spending a tremendous amount of money on a program that would have a huge impact on our companies and the military's capabilities.

We had no defined working hours; people came and went as needed, but we were on the job 24-7 that entire time. I played a predominant role in the effort, and I was a leader from out of town, so there were many eyes on me. There were some familiar people but many more who knew nothing about me. There was no job too big or too small, no task I didn't offer to lead. I didn't care if I was running out to pick up pizza for our team as we worked through the night or if I was preparing to give a project status briefing to our company executives. I was all in, no excuses, no limits. I was really loving what I was doing and couldn't get enough of it. The months passed quickly as is usually the case when you truly enjoy what you're doing.

The proposal was of such a size that we delivered it on a semitrailer from the US Southwest to the Northeast. Because of the contents, a courier who was credentialed to transport documents of a classified nature accompanied the truck. By law the proposal contents could never be outside the courier's line of sight or possession.

I had been on that job for almost eight months at that point. My daughter was due to be born at any time back home. I had lost close to twenty pounds from the work effort, stress, and poor eating and sleeping habits. I was not alone. The team had been through a lot together, and we were all in. We were so strong and together in focus there was nothing we could or would not do. There were more than one hundred dedicated team members working together for a common purpose. They were tired, and they wanted—and deserved—a break.

One of the last tasks I volunteered for was to coordinate the packaging, pickup, loading, transport, and security of the proposal's contents then its delivery to the military base in the Northeast. Most everyone else wanted to be done and return to some sense of normalcy. I could truly understand that, but there was work that remained. I estimated that the final task would take a little over a week of intense, focused effort. I built a small team, one in which all the members had volunteered to tackle those final steps in our efforts. Our team was awesome. We packed boxes, three-hole punched proposal changes and inserted them in binders, inventoried the contents, boxed up the volumes, and then loaded the trucks. Last but not least, I and a co-worker volunteered to take one complete copy of the proposal in a chase vehicle. That was necessary so just in case the primary delivery truck broke down, we could still make the delivery deadline with the backup copy. We would drive east, following the semi for nearly fifteen hundred miles just to make sure we met our delivery commitment. None of it was rocket science, and anyone who cared enough could have accomplished the final task.

On the surface we didn't do anything special. However, I was a senior leader, and it was a perfect time to set an example, to demonstrate how I appreciated and cared about our team and our collective effort. Individuals could no longer point to those of us in positions of leadership and complain about our levels of engagement or unwillingness to get our hands dirty. We prepared and delivered far more than a proposal during that period. We built and delivered to our organization a collaborative, high-performance work team by exhibiting unbounded energy and passion through our actions, not just our words. The key to unleashing energy and demonstrating your passion is to walk the walk, not just talk the talk!

Energy and passion are two soft skills I could talk about at great length. Perhaps it was the indirect challenge my father posed to me in our driveway as a young man that lit the fire I have within me. I simply refuse to approach anything I choose to do in my life with anything other than total commitment and focus. I prepare relentlessly for any challenge I face. I don't know any other way.

Is this your way? I can't make it so, but I can tell you energy and passion are contagious, attract the attention of winners, and are key components in any high-performance work culture. It's not important whether the energy and passion come from your intellect, your physical being, your emotional state, or any combination of these. It is important that your energy and passion show, that you direct them in the right way, and that they provide the desired outcomes. Find your passions and watch how fearless you can become.

I find that in most instances, we demonstrate both energy and passion together. I have so many memories from throughout my career of times when these skills served my team and me very well.

> *Sincerity is vital to enabling the full impact of energy and passion.*

Once, our chairman and our board directed me to take on a new role, leading a struggling, large business sector that was severely impacted by 9/11, a poor economy, a disease that impacted Asian air travel, and a number of internal morale and process challenges. Revenues were far below plan, margins were unacceptable, and our strategic direction was unclear. The chairman and the board gave me the the time between my taking the assignment until our next board meeting to develop a plan to turn this situation around. That was, as I recall, about six weeks!

I was a rather unknown entity among the employees in that sector, having served in a larger section of the same corporation for my entire career. Initially I focused my efforts on building my leadership team and going out and meeting all our major customers. In talking with a lot of our employees, I knew I had to have something to tell them because their anxiety levels were high. They were all important parts of the business, and they were dealing with the unknown and concerned about the future.

Once I had a good handle on what our major challenges were and what needed to be done, it was time to share the plan with all of them. I got up in front of the entire employee population, both live and via video teleconference to accommodate the employees who worked at our other locations. It was my first and best chance for them to meet me and get a feel for who I was and what my thoughts were. I had to be on top of my game.

I shared with them my initial observations. I also focused on the roles of the leadership team and the employees, setting expectations for them and me, sharing my vision for our business. The energy and passion grew as the discussion continued. I felt like I was talking directly to each employee versus reading words off a screen. I shared with them where I saw our business going and gave them my commitment to be there for them as we worked together to turn the business around. I told them if they chose to play roles in helping the business reach its full potential, we were going to have a lot of fun doing it together. If they were not up to the challenge, I would help them find employment elsewhere.

That was serious, and its magnitude was large. I wanted to fill my team with individuals who shared my vision and wanted to be part of something very special. As the discussion progressed, I could see significant changes in their attitudes and levels of engagement. The questions and comments began to flow, and I could really sense we were on our way. I can tell you that while what I had to say was interesting, it was the energy and passion that accompanied each and every word that lit the business turnaround on fire. The positive momentum continued to build, carried it's way into the hearts, minds, and the actions of our team and nineteen months later, after a huge amount of sacrifice, effort, and commitment, we were performing beyond expectations and set the stage for several more years of profitable growth.

Having passion is such an incredible feeling. It gives us energy and motivates us and those around us. Regardless of what you are passionate about, having passion can make a huge impact on how you live your life and how influential you can be. Work hard to find your passions and live your life through them at every opportunity.

Confidence

This is having a sense of certainty about something in particular, like how some action would be the most effective in solving an issue. Self-confidence is having confidence in oneself. Arrogance is unmerited confidence—overconfidence. It is important to differentiate this upfront because sometimes we confuse the terms with each other.

Up to this point, our discussion has centered around taking control, holding yourself accountable, and developing your skill base. As you do that, you naturally develop confidence. In turn you, will start to demonstrate to those around you a solid, stable,

surefooted demeanor. The concept of self-awareness comes heavily into play here. Knowing who you are and what you believe
in builds confidence. Work very hard at not looking down on
yourself, or being self-deprecating; you need truly to believe in
yourself if you expect others to do so. As much as possible, keep
all negativity away, and positivity will emanate. Positivity is key to
building confidence; negativity is an impediment to it.

Also try to understand that things won't always go the way
you prefer or expect them to go. Be willing to be flexible and
adapt, which will build confidence. I suggest you also work on
your decision-making skills to help you develop confidence.
Individuals who are troubled with indecision usually lack high
levels of self-confidence. Preparation is key. Put yourself in a
position to gather all the facts, solicit the opinions of others
when needed, and make decisions that are in the best interests
of the whole.

People gravitate to decisiveness, which builds both individual
and organizational confidence. Another thing to be cognizant
of is your body language. While this is more natural for some
than for others, it is important that we work hard to maintain
more balance in displaying our outward emotions. Of course, it
is fine to display emotion in a bounded and appropriate manner,
but in the big picture, an individual who can best control his or
her emotions and emanate stability has a far better chance of
having that same effect on others.

Another suggestion for building your confidence is to take
more risk. Playing to your strengths is smart but not at the
expense of avoiding taking on new challenges. You don't know
what you are capable of in reality until you're truly tested. Try
things you don't think you can do.

I would like to share one last suggestion that has worked well
for me in certain circumstances. I have noticed when people

have asked me to help them with issues or teach them more about certain concepts, in an indirect way they were building my level of confidence. Their inquiries bolstered my sense of purpose almost immediately. Eveyone likes to add value and usually reacts positively when asked for assistance. I suggest you be on the lookout for opportunities to ask others to teach you and for you to teach others. Confidence levels are likely to rise for both sides as a result of this simple action. Work hard to learn from and not fear failure. It's easier said than done, but it will very likely work for you.

Approachability

This competency speaks to how well we can relate to one another. Putting others at ease in order to connect and communicate more easily is the key here.

Arrogance is an undesirable form of confidence.

I have learned over time that if people are comfortable around you, feel they can have your undivided attention, and feel they can tell you what you need to know, your effectiveness improves to a great degree. I have always made time for anyone, employee or otherwise. Many times it has created scheduling challenges, but I take that chance. I always want my team to know I am there for them. That does not always translate to agreeing with them or encouraging them to avoid talking more with their direct supervisors; it's simply an opportunity to talk, share, learn, and develop as a team. I have also found that for the most part, people do not take advantage of how generous I am with my time.

One other thing I should mention here: pursuing opportunities to directly interact with others has allowed me to directly follow up on any commitments I made in the course of any prior discussions I may have had with an individual. Nothing breeds a reciprocal feeling of commitment like you actually doing what you said you would do. In parallel, it actually makes it more difficult for them to act in any other way. You can see the impact this could have on building a high-performing culture.

A great way to be more approachable is to treat others as you wish to be treated—the golden rule. Go out and approach others proactively as often as possible. Become the one people see out there, the one who reaches out to others. Over time their comfort in approaching you will increase. When they do approach, make the discussions more about them. Show interest in them, and remember it is not always about you. Another tip is to spend some time walking around and finding oppurtunities to interact with others. Your visibility is really key here.

We all have our rough edges; no one is perfect. Do your best to be at your best when interacting. Try hard to be as polite, attentive, and sensitive as possible. This will build your level of approachability. Always encourage others to build their levels of confidence; everyone loves to be encouraged. Always keep to yourself what others tell you in confidence. If you want people to avoid you, break their trust in you. Once that happens, the chances of recovering a good relationship will decrease.

Remember, it will take time to develop these skills. Make this all part of your operating style. Be consistent and persistent, and have fun along the way.

Responsibility and Accountability

We often use these two words interchangeably, but there is a difference. Responsibility is taking ownership. Accountability is a process of making, keeping, and managing agreements and expectations in any relationship and making a commitment to accept the consequences of ones actions.

As I have noted, your development starts with being responsible for yourself and the outcomes of your actions. How can you expect that in others if you truly can't demonstrate it in yourself? By this I mean taking responsibility for the role you played on a project or assignment in which performance fell short. Because you were responsible for the project, you must hold yourself accountable for the results. What could you have done differently when things didn't go as planned? It is easier to blame others and shrug off your role, but in doing that you will greatly impede your team members' desires to have your back when you need it most. Be quick to congratulate them on a job well done versus using success as an opportunity to advertise your own worth. Let the performance of the organization speak for itself, and in the meantime, be responsible for everything that happens within your purview, always having the best interests of your team at the top of your list.

Even early on in my career, there were times when the ramifications of falling short of a duty or making a mistake could have been significant. Perhaps it was my supervisors' adversity to risk that led me to be less willing to accept accountability. Or maybe it was because I felt, rightly or wrongly, that our work environment was quite risk averse and intolerant of mistakes, and that impeded my affinity for accountability. As a person who spent a large amount of time managing many projects of all sizes, I ran into the responsibility and accountability dynamic almost daily. While I always felt I had the responsilbity to lead, I can't truthfully say I always owned the results. Blaming others and protecting my own interests was not uncommon earlier in my career. I learned through the help of my many mentors that building trust and having the confidence and desire to do what it takes to win in life were instrumental in my personal development. Accepting accountability for my actions and for the actions of those I led was critical to generating a highly collaborative and committed team.

Try to think of it like this: the best way to motivate yourself to overcome development challenges or performance shortcomings is to be held accountable. If there are no consequences, from where will the motivation to change come? Individuals who can be accountable to themselves first will be more receptive to others holding them accountable. While this can come over time with maturity, placing an emphasis on this early in your journey is a very useful practice.

Knowing who you are accountable to and understanding the consequences are key factors. Truly understanding, accepting, and embracing accountability as one way to fuel your development are all important things to remember. Your objective here is to become comfortable with accountability early on and practice it regularly; it will then become an instrumental part of who you are, and it will surely serve to help build the strength of your character along the way. My transition did not occur overnight, but with focus and emphasis it did happen, and it played a huge role in my development.

Vision

This is defined as a desired future state of direction. In that sense you can relate to one definition of a leader as a person who takes an individual or an entire organization to a place it would not go on its own. For many of us, it is always easier to focus on the more tactical issues in front of us.

> *To be in charge means to be responsible and accountable.*

We can see the issue, take the time to understand it, and take action to deal with it. There is usually a great sense of accomplishment in doing this. Results are usually quickly realized, and this encourages us to reenforce that behavior through emphasizing a tactical focus even more.

A more complicated and less tangible skill that in many cases separates the leaders from the followers is the unique ability to sit back and assess the bigger picture. In some cases, not everything is well defined or even understood; there may be no insight as to what's right or wrong. The desired outcome is speculative and unclear, and the path to get from where you are now to that future state has not yet been defined. For example, keeping an organization in a position to compete effectively and grow profitably in any market condition requires a long-term strategic perspective. The senior leaders in the organization typically drive the process. In a collaborative environment, they set the long-term performance objectives; the other parts of the organization then embrace and implement the strategies in order to turn the vision into reality within a specific time frame. I have seen many capable managers limit their abilities to achieve their full potential because they did not adequately address this critical skill.

What if you are not in a position to have this opportunity or are in an environment where this opportunity doesn't exist? There are still so many things you can do to stimulate the visionary within you.

I first suggest you spend more time thinking about what could be—it's invigorating. Getting away from focusing on only the moment or what's expected will be a first great step. Next, I believe, thinking about the longer-term puts a further degree of importance on what's immediate and the big role that plays in moving forward. Using your passion both internally and externally will go a long way toward moving many to act.

Patience—to a point—is also important here. Big ideas are difficult at times to develop; once you've thought them out, implementation and acceptance are usually not quick. Have the staying power to stand behind what you believe in, and do all you can to keep your ideas alive.

I suggest you try hard not to accept readily what others have defined the future to be. While it sounds a bit cliché, the best way to predict the future is to do all you can to create it. If your organization has a business development or strategic management function, do what you can to get involved in some form of strategy creation at the appropriate level. Start simply by thinking about the things that could either enable or impede your efforts to achieve your vision. Then start thinking about the impact they would have on your current state. Also, begin to think about what you're going to do about it. Being actively involved in activities that will expose you to the development and implementation of a strategic plan will go a long way toward getting you started. You will need to work hard at making the time to do this because usually we tend to the more pressing tactical needs of our daily lives first.

You will recall that in chapter one I wrote about the impact our landing on the moon had on me as a child. President Kennedy's speech announcing the event on May 25, 1961, was based on his vision to escalate our focus on space travel and to land a man on the moon before the end of the decade. This can give you a sense of why sometimes stretching your thinking far out of your comfort zone is so powerful. If entire generations can be inspired by goals some viewed as impossible, what can the impact be on much smaller groups or individuals? Vision encourages us to think and act in time frames that outdate us and our current way of thinking about things. It also encourages us to look at solutions that are, in most cases, quite far from the obvious, sometimes referred to as critical thinking. This is a skill that has such tremendous utility and is not easily acquired. To begin, please accept the fact that it takes no more effort to create huge, game-changing opportunities than to identify small, near-term objectives. It's all about how you direct your time and whether being truly challenged inspires you. The other reality is that it is more difficult for some to think in these longer terms with far less definition while facing the reality that there are many unknowns that could impact the outcome. But you see, at the same time that's the attraction, and why the skill set is treasured and exactly why many cower away from developing it.

The business sector I was leading in the later stages of my career had achieved some success in improving our domestic market growth rates, but our international presence and revenue lagged behind the market outlook. As part of our strategic plan, we made expanding our international footprint a top priority. We recognized that the US Department of Defense's spending was going to experience extreme budget pressure, so we needed to find growth in other markets. That move would not only offer potential revenue and margin expansion, but also serve to counter the rather cyclical nature of our commercial domestic markets and, if successful, provide increased shareholder value.

We developed a vision that on paper showed a plan where our international revenues could potentially exceed the revenues of our domestic business in a five-year time frame. At that time, however, we were far from that point, and achieving that objective seemed next to impossible. Talking about it was not enough; there were the challenges of market knowledge, physical presence, customer relationships, investment needs, time to market, and competitive response, to name just a few. But, as with any strategy, our team developed collaboratively the supportive goals and objectives, and the journey began.

I took responsibility for strategy implementation and became a very visible ambassador for our focus on it. I made significant changes in what I spent my time doing. That created more opportunity for me to be directly involved by delegating domestic and tactical-related efforts to others around me, which supported their growth and development.

We traveled quite often to the regions we targeted. We applied the cultural learnings many team members had gained and began to create relationships with key decision makers. In that way we developed a far sharper sense of the competitive landscape and what the customers truly wanted. We began to understand what it would take to prevail! We built a team; we invested in people, technology, infrastructure, and time. We made trade-offs based on strategic importance, and, in each and every case, we walked the walk rather than just talking the talk. We were appropriately patient and had staying power to maintain focus when the market trends softened for short peroids.

It took several years, but we evolved that sector to become far more balanced in its business composition, and the growth we achieved continues to serve the company very well to this date. In doing all of that, we taught many people the importance of strategy, the art of focus, the powers of energy and passion, the strength of collaboration, the ability to think big, and the criticality

It takes no more time to look far into the future than to stare in the present, and that's a lot more exciting.

of staying power. We walked the walk and never relented. This is exactly how one leads others and puts them in a position to be a part of something truly amazing. It's more than just words. It's all about actions—*your* actions—and the examples you set for yourself and everyone with whom you interact.

Embracing Change

This skill is complex as well because it calls for you to question *why* and *how* you and others continue to do something in the same way you have been doing it forever. Many people are anxious over the idea of change, and to a great extent, those who have not been exposed to a culture of change feel quite threatened by it. These are both common and natural reactions to any change process.

For an individual or a business not only to survive but remain competitive and prosper, they must understand and master the skill of embracing change. Disciplining yourself in your own domain, always looking for a better way, while in parallel, knowing you may fail and have to start over is complex enough. Now imagine the challenges of leading an organization through change and needing to deal with all the individual and group dynamics that come along with it. To be successful here, you will need to apply many of the soft skills we have discussed. With that, don't let the risk and difficulty of the associated tasks scare you away.

Embracing change is the skill that really posed a huge challenge for me. I was used to doing things my way, and the results were usually quite positive. Why change? I could not see the reason; the case for change was not clear. Then my supervisors reminded me that we were in a highly competitive market, and our customers had choices. What we brought to the marketplace had to be different, be more competitive, and provide our customers with a better-value proposition than that of our competitors. If that did not occur, we would lose, and the stakes were huge.

I read and studied a lot about the change process. With the help of my mentors, I learned to examine myself and to understand and face my fears and apprehensions. I also learned to look beyond myself and my own comfort levels and recognized that the world does not stand still for anyone. If you embrace change, you will soon find yourself reenergized as you explore new ways to accomplish great results. There are entire books and processes dedicated to the subject of the importance of change. And I could not see my discussion of soft skills not including the concept of change; it is that vital.

Another way to help you better understand the dynamics here is to take you inside my transformation. First, please believe that what I went through in a corporate setting applies in every aspect to each and every one of us. It's the larger lessons we learn that span all professional and personal situations we find ourselves in at this point in time or in the future. It really has very little to do with the setting in which we learn the lessons.

Our chairman was a visionary, and he embraced change, always driving for continuous improvement. He despised the status quo and was constantly looking for ways to differentiate our company from others. His big ideas were always accompanied by a need to do things differently as the idea matured through implementation.

The markets we served were cyclical, and the need to anticipate those cycles and their impact on our ability to compete effectively was crucial to our success. The chairman developed an organizational concept that in his mind was entirely driven toward improving our operating performance in each aspect of our value chain. That efficiency would contribute to improving the value we would be able to pass on to our customers; it would also improve our competitive position, drive revenue growth, better leverage our finacial and human resources, and improve the resulting profit margins.

As he began to share and refine his thoughts, our chairman brought his leadership team together off-site to solicit members' views and—equally important—test our level of support for the concepts. Well, I will tell you that initially the reactions were a mixed bag. I could see the dividing lines developing right before my eyes. In spite of the tremendous job the chairman did in defining the reason for change and the benefits that our customers, employees, and stockholders would realize, many team members weren't listening. Those who saw it as an opportunity to gain influence, authority, or power tended to support the concept. Those who felt they were going to be on the losing end of the change clearly were not embracing the idea.

I quickly came to the conclusion that I would lose control, authority, responsibility, and the ability to make an impact. I took it personally from the very beginning. That perspective was based primarily on emotion, and I did not allow myself to reflect without bias on the facts and absorb the need for change. All my barriers were up in full force, and it was apparent. I know why I never was very good at playing poker: my body language and the manner and content of my role in the discussions said everything I was thinking. A visible and respected senior leader openly resisting change does nothing to gain the confidence and support of the employees.

The chairman saw all of that going on and was not at all pleased. He tried more group dialogue but quickly concluded that it was time for a more direct approach. He solicited the support of those who were not visibly resistant and led the charge on those of us who were. It became very clear that while he was open to debate and discussion, he was determined the change was going to occur with or without our support.

The moment of truth came when he asked me to come to his office for a chat. He got right to the point. He let me know he had noticed my attitude and was very concerned about how my shadow of leadership was impacting the employees' affinity for his ideas. While he clearly recognized my status, potential, and contribution to the company, no one was going to question his concept and negatively influence its eventual implementation—particularly not any members of his leadership team.

He did exactly the right thing at exactly the right time. I did not say much, but I listened very intensely. I left the office knowing I had a decision to make. It was clear the organizational change was going to happen with or without me playing a part in it. I worked hard to understand the facts and worked equally hard to keep my emotions out of the picture. That was not easy, but I managed the best I could.

I discussed the concept with others in the organization who had diverse perspectives on it, so I could get a good idea of how others who were in the know felt. I then questioned each and every aspect of the change I had originally found threatening. In each case I worked really hard to find an offsetting benefit or opportunity. To be honest, I was not totally successful, but it gave me a more balanced position. All of that was not easy for me. My pride and ego were impediments. I found I was placing too much importance on how the change would supposedly impact my effectiveness as a leader and not nearly enough on trying to understand and buy-in to the advertised benefits.

I worked hard at it all, as it was a huge step in the evolution of our company. Over time my attitude began to shift from dissention to support and finally to becoming an advocate. Don't get me wrong—I would *not* have become an advocate due to personal and political pressures. I would have left the organization before I'd ever have done that. You may very well find yourself in that position because in reality not every big idea is accepted unanimously. You will have your own choices to make. If you do as I have described, your path for making the best choice, all things considered, will be far more enjoyable than my first real challenge of embracing change was.

While you are assessing your skill sets and talking to mentors, peers, and others in your network, it is easy to focus on the more tangible hard skill sets. Many people are most comfortable dealing in that realm. I ask you not to let that limit your development. Individuals and leaders at all levels do many things, but above all, they lead themselves and others to places they won't go on their own. It is your responsibility to bring out the very best in yourself, and, in time, to be in a position to help others around you reach their full potential. In order to do this, you must understand the human resource as fully as you can. You will need to know how to organize, motivate, and inspire yourself as well as others to go above and beyond and do so willingly, with a high degree of energy, passion, and commitment. Your objective is to get others to do what is necessary in a collaborative fashion to convert vision into action and reality. You must learn to do this at every level—starting, of course, with yourself.

So how can I help you deal with embracing change more easily? First, work hard to deal only with the facts. People spend countless hours fretting over the rumor mills filled with unsubstantiated concerns that those who resist change invent. Seek out the sponsor(s) of the change and work hard to determine reality from fallacy.

While it is natural and human nature to start personalizing what impact the change will have on you, the outcome can go one of two ways. One is to let all your concerns and fears take over, so you spend your time dealing with negativity. The other way is to imagine the possibilities and find ways to drive the outcome to provide some tangible benefit to you and others. Look for the positive, and be as opportunistic as possible at every chance you can. Work hard not to be simply the victim and accept what comes your way; I suggest that it's far better to get involved, voice your concerns, and become part of the solution.

Finally, I suggest that in doing this, you become an advocate for continuous change. You need to understand that time stands still for no one, and change will be continuous in all aspects of our lives. The future is inherently unknown. To get there from the present, we must understand that change will always be a major component of that evolution.

I simply ask you to be brave and bold, take full advantage of all the opportunities a changing environment will offer you, and adapt quickly to many of the unexpected circumstances you will face along the way. You really don't have a choice unless you choose to get left behind.

In closing out this discussion on soft skills, let me leave you with some additional things to consider. Please work hard to recognize and accept the fact that developing these skill sets is quite instrumental in learning how to become more effective in dealing with diverse situations.

Becoming more competent in these types of skills sets will enable us all to become even more self-aware as well as aware of how we can best apply all we are and what we have to offer in any given circumstance.

As an employer I can tell you, without reservation, that the importance of these skills is very significant, and in most if not all cases they can serve as key differentiators when making hiring decisions at all levels.

If you take full advantage of what I have offered here, you will see your effectivity climb to new levels. This I can say quite confidently!

CHAPTER 8

THE SHADOW OF LEADERSHIP

I want you to take a step away from skills now as I attempt to shed some light on behaviors I believe are both relevant and essential to any discussion about personal and professional development. Skills are crucial, but alone they are not enough. When I speak of behavior, I am specifically talking about how you carry yourself throughout your personal and professional lives—how you act and how others see you in particular situations.

It is not enough simply to possess a long list of hard skills in which you are competent to varying degrees. I further contend that it is not enough to possess certain soft skills even when combined with a robust list of hard skills. To be a thoroughly outfitted leader, taking into account how you act whether others are around or not will have quite a prolific impact on your effectiveness. That's right: how others see you, even from afar, speaks volumes about who you are and what you stand for—perhaps without your ever having to say a single word. I have chosen to define this as the leadership shadow you cast.

I believe the behaviors that define an individual can be learned over time through observation, coaching, and practice. This applies to each and every one of us regardless of our personality types or the types and numbers of skill sets we possess. One of the keys here is to mold your observations and teachings so they adapt well given your personality type. A very outgoing, gregarious personality may find it more natural to project a high level of confidence; whether it is genuine or not is another matter. Yet that same individual may be more challenged than his or her more reserved peers or associates when it comes to emitting a level of calmness when faced with a challenging circumstance. At times people draw conclusions on a single, brief observation of others that in many cases could be as inaccurate as it could be dead on. My points here are simple: be cognizant of the shadow you cast, and learn over time to recognize that the larger your network and the more visible you become, the degree of importance and effectiveness your shadow carries is heightened.

Sometimes you learn some of life's most valuable lessons through unplanned circumstances or experiences that were not at all anticipated. In many instances I have the need to see things for myself, and while I had no idea what was about to occur, I once had an experience at work that made an indelible impression on me that will last forever.

I was having a challenging workday. My team and I had just learned that the federal government had made huge funding cuts to a series of programs on which our organization was working. The impacts of those cuts would be substantial in terms of revenue reduction. I also knew it would likely cause us to have to reduce our employment accordingly. Laying people off, while necessary, was the most difficult task I faced as a leader; just the *possibility* of facing a reduction in workforce was very concerning.

A series of program-performance challenges happened to be uncovered that day as well, and they always got my attention. All of that weighed heavily on my mind. I told my assistant I was going for a walk to clear my mind and think a bit outside my office. I told her I would be back in a short time.

As I walked around the facility, I thought about the challenges we were facing as a business and began to formulate in my mind what I would do about them. I was really focused. After about fifteen minutes, I went back to my office, sat down, and continued with the tasks at hand. My assistant came to me a short time after I returned and said I had a call on hold from a person I had known for years and with whom I had worked closely over an extended period. I took the call.

His first words were, "Bob, are you upset with me?"

I responded, "Absolutely not, why would you think that?"

He retorted, "You just walked by my office. Your head was down, the intense look on your face was chilling, and you didn't acknowledge my greeting!"

Wow, I thought, *are you kidding me?* He noticed all of that in a brief glance and drew the conclusion that I was angry with him! What had I done? How could he think that? I'll tell you how. He had seen the angst on my face, the intensity of my stride, the uncharacteristically cold nature, and my lack of greeting. He felt comfortable enough reaching out to me, which was huge. In his doing so, I learned a significant lesson. What about the others who had seen similar things but didn't take the time to call me? What did *they* think? Word travels fast and "opinions" are formed quickly, believe me!

My point here is: always remember that the image you cast to others, knowingly or unknowingly, can send messages to them that you may or may not want sent. Try to be more cognizant of this as you develop and grow.

Let's begin a discussion about several important behavioral characteristics.

Ethics and Integrity

In my view, any discussion about core behaviors must start with

The image you cast to others is like reading a book about yourself out loud.

understanding the meanings of the terms *ethics* and *integrity*. First you need to appreciate that while these words are often used interchangeably, there is a huge difference! *Ethics* is used to define a set of values, rules, policies, or procedures that govern the conduct of a particular group of individuals. There are business ethics that govern what is allowable conduct in a specific business environment—things such as procurement rules, hiring practices, and other behavioral guidelines. There are medical ethics that govern the behaviors of those serving in the health care industry—practices such as treatment protocols and costs would be examples. So *ethics* can, in short, be defined simply as "the rules."

Integrity has a very different meaning, although it goes hand in hand with ethics. *Integrity* relates to how we carry ourselves, how we act, and how we behave in certain circumstances. Most of the time, there are guidelines or ethics in place to govern our actions. To me, integrity means doing the right thing each and every time without condition or compromise.

When I think of integrity, I can't help but think of words like *brave* and *bold*. Why? Because sometimes, in both the professional and personal aspects of our lives, it takes being these two things to do the right thing in spite of the consequences. This does not come easily for everyone because we are all driven by different motivations. A doctor focused on maximizing revenue at the expense of appropriate patient care is one example. How about a business leader who places their personal accountability at a higher priority than following the procurement integrity practices in order to grow the business at any cost? These two simple examples illustrate that integrity is all about our behaviors. We decide how we act in certain circumstances whether anybody else is watching or not; it's our choice alone.

With all our talk about taking control of your life and being responsible for your developmental success, it should be said that this must not come at the expense of prostituting your personal and professional integrity—*ever*. In my role as an employer and team builder throughout my career, I never compromised when seeking individuals who demonstrated integrity. It just so happens that over time, people become more like those around them, which in turn defines the character of the environment. If you want a culture where integrity is an instrumental part, you can never make any exceptions. This applies in your own actions, your selection of people, and your adherence to holding everyone accountable for their behavior. Individual and business success will come and go, as it's a natural outcome of a free market environment where the rules of survival of the fittest apply; but integrity is forever regardless of everything else.

You must understand that individuals as well as organizations that are not well-founded in integrity will ultimately fail. You don't want anything to do with an organization or individuals that operate without ethical integrity. Strive to play a huge role, not only by becoming all you can, but also by doing it the right way. The media is filled with examples of individuals, groups, and large corporations that have violated state, federal, or even international policies that govern ethical behavior. The consequences can be dire. Aside from the overall economic impact on the business, the impact on reputation and the collateral damage that extends to everyone even marginally associated with it lives on forever.

Initially it would appear you have two choices here. The first is to be part of an organization that places a tremendous amount of emphasis on integrity, ethics, and standards of business conduct. The next choice you have is even more personal: How do you intend to do your part and all you can to ensure your actions and behaviors represent the values of the enterprise? Your values reflect an image for others to observe, follow, and pass on. Don't be fooled. In the end you really have only one choice here, and it's quite simple. You must always choose to do the right thing without exception or compromise—*always*.

Learning about doing the right thing hopefully started at the very beginning of your existence, but it will continually be challenged each and every day of your life. When you live by these principles daily and set examples for others to follow, you will see how this most important behavior will define everything. Who you are personally and professionally and how others view you defines who you are in their eyes.

One last thought on ethics and integrity: I view it as table stakes—no real choice and no compromise. Adhering to doing what's right is an essential and expected behavior. However, once that has been compromised, there is never any complete recovery. It's an indelible stain and tarnish. Simply put, you must always do the right thing.

> *Doing what is right can be challenging even to the best of us.*

Walking the Walk

Surely you have heard this: "He can talk the talk, but can he walk the walk?" The latter means doing what you say you are going to do—putting your words into action—as opposed to "talking the talk," which means *saying* you are going to do something but not doing it.

While it's quite easy to say you'll do something, demonstrating this behavior in a consistent manner over an extended period is by far a bigger challenge. This is all about personal credibility and people's reliance on your word. For some people, making excuses may seem valid to explain why they did not fulfill some commitment, but in many cases it seems to be a way for people to rationalize to themselves and others why they didn't step up. That's a hard impression to erase once it's established, but it's never too late to focus on doing what you say you're going to do—that is, walking the walk.

Some would call me a risk taker, an individual who will go to extremes to get things done and done correctly by doing it the right way. While it may appear that at times my actions are not prudent, I can tell you that is not the case. Drawing upon my intuition, values, experiences, and gut feelings when making decisions in challenging circumstances has continually served me well.

One day I was in a hospital having another follow-up surgery on that severely broken ankle I told you about in the introduction to this book. The early morning surgery lasted about three hours, and I was recovering in my hospital room when the phone rang. It was the chairman of my company, and he was calling for two purposes. First, he wanted to know how I was doing. He also wanted to be clear on who would be representing me at an upcoming briefing for those in leadership on embracing change.

Sound familiar? This event was an instrumental part of our journey to change and enhance our business and its culture. It was our chance to talk to our leadership team about our plans. The stakes were huge, as we were talking about transforming the company. I had prepared my remarks for that event, so my being ready was never a question. I had briefly thought about a backup plan should I not be able to deliver the thoughts myself, knowing the surgery was imminent, but I had not given that idea much thought. So when he asked me who would be representing my interests, I told him I would.

Now, I have failed to mention that the briefing was later that afternoon. As we spoke, I was on a morphine drip and intravenous fluids, and had a catheter to assist me with my obligations to nature. The chairman and I debated my decision, but, as was always the case, he trusted that either I or someone else would follow through as committed. Of course he was naturally concerned about the risk to my health attending the event presented, but he left the choice of personally participating up to me.

After hanging up, I thought, *what the hell am I going to do?* There was no way the doctor would release me. At the same time, there was no way I wasn't going to do it myself. I had made a commitment. The topic was crucial. I would need to cast my shadow of leadership large, and I refused to make any excuses for my inability to participate. I am sure my company's employees would have understood had I decided to delegate my role to another leader, but instead I chose to do it myself. Recall our discussion of my struggling with embracing change? That was another opportunity to demonstrate my level of personal buy-in.

So I devised what I believed to be the greatest escape. I called one of the senior leaders in my financial organization and asked her to bring some planning information to the hospital for my review. I asked her to come about forty-five minutes before the time of the briefing. In the interim, after the nurses made their rounds, I pulled out the IVs and shut off the alarms. Having been a medic in the service, I knew how to remove a catheter. I cut my pant leg open to accommodate my cast, put my shirt on, got my crutches, picked a time when the nurses were preoccupied at their station, and waited right by the elevator. As soon as she arrived, I got into the elevator and punched the button for the parking level.

I tried to explain my plan to her, but she was shocked and upset about being an involuntary accomplice to my escape. I wasn't buying in to her pleas to reconsider. She drove me to the venue, and we walked in together. There were several hundred people in attendance. It was mandatory for all leaders, and, as a result, it was mandatory for me as well—no excuses.

You should have seen the reactions, the looks on their faces, and the chatter! I know they were questioning my sanity. Hell, they were right; it was way over the top, but I had weighed the risks and felt the trade-offs were worth it. I was confident I could keep the weight off my foot to minimize the swelling and felt good about my ability to think clearly and deliver my message effectively. Focusing and controlling the things I could impact was the name of the game. I felt very good about my decision to proceed; otherwise, I would not have participated in the event. That was my choice, and it had come about after a lot of thought.

It was one of my most effective briefings, but aside from that, what a series of signals I sent to the masses about the degree of importance I placed on that effort! The company was asking them to make commitments to the business and to us, the leadership, so it only followed that I should stand behind my commitment to them. Word traveled fast throughout the organization, and while it was far from being the only reason for our successful journey, it was hard to argue the impact that entire meeting had on our success and our employees' attitudes about embracing change and doing what they say they're going to do.

Life is filled with the unexpected. I am not talking about instances that are totally beyond our control, that impact our abilities to do what we say we will. My recommendation in those cases is very simple: accept it fully and do all you can to make it right. The signals you send to others by behaving this way will, as always, serve as a powerful example and relate directly to them your expectations of them.

Being honest is also a tremendously important aspect of fulfilling your commitments. "No" is sometimes not only the best answer but the *only* answer. When you know *why* you're saying no, doing so indicates a sense of confidence. It is a display of self-respect and respect for others by not selling yourself out for a short instant by making yourself feel good and avoiding conflict, all the while knowing what you have committed to is simply not possible.

One final thought on walking the walk. There are many who believe we should never commit to anything unless we are totally convinced, without any doubt, that it can be done. While I understand and respect this philosophy, I do not subscribe to it. If I feel there is a chance something is possible, I make a commitment and use the challenge to motivate my team and myself. Yes, sometimes we fall short and have to make it right. But remember, it's not about always being right or batting 100 percent. It is about always putting forth your best effort! I also recognize that your ability to make things right becomes more difficult in a smaller environment where your flexibility may be limited and your capability to absorb mistakes is less robust. In this instance you can only do your best.

Being true to your word always, and without condition or excuse, is the only way. Once people around you notice this behavior, and it becomes synonymous with your name, you are well on your way to becoming a successful leader at any level.

Staying in the Moment

This concept has many connotations in both our personal and professional lives. Since this book is primarily about development, I will steer clear of talking about how to live for today, living in the present, and so on. To be clear, what I am referring to here is simply this: remain-

> *Do what you say, or do everything you can to make it right.*

ing focused on the task at hand. More specifically, when you are dealing directly with people individually or in group settings, you must do all you can to provide them with your complete and undivided attention. While this seems obvious to many, it is a rule many do not follow. Not being in the moment puts you in a position of losing out on learning something and missing out on important and interesting events. In diverting your attention away from those in your presence, you are sending a strong signal that what they have to offer is unimportant to you. Whether or not it is intentional is not the point, nor does it matter. In this day and age, when our smartphones and other PDAs are always in our hands, staying in the know through the use of social networking is a constant temptation. The ability to remain focused is challenging, and more often than not our obsessive desire to remain connected hinders it.

I am not advocating that you not take part in social networking. I am, however, strongly suggesting you stay connected to the moment and remain focused on the task at hand with the individuals you are engaged with at the time. Have you ever been in a conversation with someone and another individual who was not originally involved rudely interrupts? Of course you have. Or perhaps you have been the one doing the interrupting. I have been in both positions. How did you feel? Unimportant? Did you feel that what you had to say was not interesting, valid, or pertinent? Don't send the unintended signal to others that what they have to offer is not germane because you are not focusing on the task at hand. Rather, remain focused, listen intently as others speak, and share and ask follow-up questions if something being discussed remains unclear. When people feel they have your undivided attention, you are once again building their self-confidence and self-respect.

Diversity

What comes to your mind when you hear the word *diversity*? For many in my generation, equality of race and ethnicity is a prevalent thought. The fact remains that the population composition trends in the United States indicate that in fewer than forty years from now, there will be no majority group represented in our country either ethnically or racially. What does that say about the meaning of diversity in our lives and how we might view it?

If you understand and/or believe in diversity of thought as a key attribute, you know where I'm headed. If you're unfamiliar with the concept, let me give you an executive summary to make my point. In group settings, particularly those with specific foci or senses of purpose, having individuals with varying cultural legacies, experience levels, soft skill competencies, organizational relationships, and the like is key. Of course, age, ethnicity, gender, and racial diversity will follow. Why is this important? Well, what better way to push the envelope of incumbent thinking than to challenge the status quo? Creating more energy in discussions with a diverse set of individuals where creativity is key is instrumental in developing more effective outcomes.

I want very little to do with an organization that does not place a premium on creating a diverse workplace for the benefit of both its employees and its customers. I honestly believe any organization stuck in the comfort of incumbent thought will not survive. Attracting talent to come work in more uniform organizations will continue to be highly problematic. Tough market conditions have dramatic effects on the competitive landscape as each competing firm pushes to increase market share. Incumbent solutions will not excite a customer base that is likely looking for solutions that provide incremental value and that are economically attractive as well. It's simple: to be more competitive and innovative, you must have a workplace that not only encourages but rewards creativity of thought. I'm encouraging you to find ways to solve problems using teams comprised of people with different sets of experiences, beliefs, thoughts, and backgrounds.

So how is this done? It starts with a commitment to make team diversity a priority. Regardless of whether you are an individual contributor or a senior leader with extensive organizational responsibility, the same concepts apply. The scale and complexity may be different, but that doesn't matter when considering the end result. What is required is always to look for ways to engage with and surround yourself with people who don't think like you. I know that may sound easy, but in my experience that is acting in a way that is very unnatural. Our natural tendency is to align ourselves with those who think along the same lines we do. So asking us to work toward moving away from what's natural will be challenging, but it is essential.

It will be even more of a challenge to manage the group dynamic in a diverse setting because the opportunities for chaos, conflict, and disagreement will naturally increase. This is a challenge I am always willing to accept. Doing this not only provides a more creative solution environment but allows me to hone my meeting-management, communication, and decision-making skills all at the same time.

I have a quick story to help make my point. I had just taken over a new sector of a business and felt it important to visit our many locations to hold several skip-level meetings. These were designed to facilitate my interaction with all employees regardless of where they were in the organization or what titles they held. I wanted to know what was on the minds of *all* our employees.

These sessions included individuals representing all levels of leadership and all functions within the organization. My first thought was to personally lead these sessions along with my staff. While we were diverse in our own right, I felt something far more creative was needed. The composition of our workforce was changing as the ages and experience levels of our average new hires were dropping. The cultural backgrounds of our less experienced employees were far more diverse and more representative of what was occurring in the general population.

So what did I do? I developed a team through both individual selection and volunteers creating a group of employees from both headquarters and each location we planned to visit. It was a highly diverse group of individuals in every aspect: age, gender, experience, culture, function, and education. There were many reasons for doing that. I wanted to assess our challenges from a varied set of values, backgrounds, and experiences. I knew if I approached it in a more traditional sense, I would not learn as much, and it would negatively impact the utility of the exercise.

I also wanted to send a message about the importance of workplace diversity to each and every employee. I was quite impressed by how all the selected individuals stepped up and contributed in huge ways. They asked questions about issues that were important to them. There is no way that would have occurred had I followed my original plan. I was bounded by my own paradigms and as a result, our solutions would have been equally limited. We were discussing issues that were new, and their resolution required us to explore uncharted territories to develop the right responses. All of that came about through my encouraging an environment of diverse thought. Equally impressive was the manner in which the organization responded to the challenges we outlined and faced together. As a result, everyone became an instrumental part of the solution.

So what are the lessons learned here? An individual, group, or business that not only understands and recognizes but also practices diversity of thought is creating a competitive advantage. This can come in many personal and professional forms. Whether it is increased performance at an individual or business level, or the ability to offer customers and clients better-value solutions to their problems, diversity of thought is a real differentiator.

Just the opposite is true as well. More uniform environments that do not practice or engage in cultures of diversity will stagnate and disappear in time. If we don't set a tone that allows us to leverage fully the contributions and experiences of those around us, we simply won't survive. All customers in all businesses have options for whom to do business with. Encouraging all employees to become integral parts of creating solutions that offer the best values is the name of the game. Cultivate in your employees the ability to share and listen to diverse viewpoints. Practice active listening. Facilitate constructive debate in which perspectives widely differ. Be decisive. Chances are you will not make everyone happy, nor will you always achieve 100 percent unanimity. That's not the objective. The goal is always to strive for the best possible outcome, and practicing diversity of thought is a crucial behavior for making this a reality.

Concern for Others

This point is twofold: demonstrating a genuine concern for others and practicing the art of humility. First, the importance of demonstrating a genuine concern for others on a consistent basis is huge. We can all relate to how we feel when we are in the presence of someone who truly

Diversity is so much more than gender, race, and religion.

cares about our well-being. Whether it's in an individual or a group setting, whether it's in a personal or professional environment, its applicability and impact remain. Recall our discussion in chapter three about mentoring and what characteristics to look for when selecting a mentor: you want someone who truly cares and is excited about the role. The same behavior concept applies here. Exuding a caring attitude will go a long way toward creating a committed, collaborative, energized, and compassionate setting that will be exhilarating for all involved.

There are so many stories I would love to share with you at this point to demonstrate this concept of caring. But let me tell you one that to this day lives steadfastly in my heart. We all face challenges in our lives; no one is exempt. While at times these challenges seem overwhelming and insurmountable, you must remember you are not alone. And while there are times when facing your challenges alone may be prudent, more often than not a helping hand from someone who truly cares can have a lot of impact.

Over the years my largest challenge has been my family's battle with cancer. I lost my grandmother to the disease when I was a younger man, and my mom recently lost her battle later in her life. My wife was diagnosed with stage IV cancer several years ago and continues her brave fight to survive daily. So cancer is something I have experienced, studied, and know a little about, and as a result, my awareness of the disease is keen.

While at work I learned of two employees over a relatively short period of time, who were battling the disease in two different ways. One had stage IV breast cancer that had spread to her brain. The other had a young daughter who was stricken with a rare form of the disease. The prognosis was not good in either case. So there I was leading a large business, and through my large network I had become aware of those employees' challenges. I had several options. I could ignore what they were going through and privately wish the best for them. Or I could try to make a difference. I chose the latter. I did not get involved for my own sake, though doing so did make me feel more complete. I did it because I truly cared about those people and could relate directly to their situations. I knew I could make a difference—the same difference that others who reached out to me had made in improving my ability to cope with the challenges of life.

I went to visit both employees separately at their workstations, unannounced. While I had not met those two women, I was aware of who they were and what roles each played on our team. They knew me only by my title and face. I found them both working diligently, but their concerns about the unknown were apparent. The woman with metastasized breast cancer didn't have a long time to live, and she told me about the things she wished she had done. She had always wanted to find a way to visit her son out east, maybe have an opportunity to attend his dental school graduation and see her grandchildren, but she had always thought she could not afford to be away from work because her financial situation was fragile. Now, with her health challenges, she felt that was no longer possible.

I told her to pack up her things, gave her a full, paid leave of absence, and got her tickets to go see her family out east. She left that day, did all the things she had wished for and shared with me, and never came back to work. I was so happy I had taken the opportunity to help her in some small way and to bring her some comfort during her final time on Earth.

I did all I could to make life a bit easier for the other employee. I, along with her supervisor, really encouraged her to focus more time and energy on her daughter's health and family related challenges and did what we could to help put her work related concerns on the back burner. Even though in both cases the outcome resulted in a loss of life, I know how much these small actions meant to my team members. To this day, I get emotional as I recall our dialogues and their relief at learning I truly cared. Word traveled fast throughout our company that the hard-nosed, high-energy, passionate leader had a heart. Even today, others who have heard about this along the way remind me of those acts of kindness.

All I ask is that you stay aware, get involved, and make differences in others' lives by showing them you truly care. My words cannot do this justice. Pass it on!

Humility

Let's now turn our attention to the behavior we all know as humility. Simply stated, it means being modest and respectful. In my experience, the more at ease I and others became with parking our egos and coming to terms with our humility, the more our effectiveness improved. I am talking about a genuine demonstration of

> *It's not what you did for others that is important; it is important that you cared.*

humility here, not veneer, not the false or episodic kind and a genuine and consistent demonstration of choosing humility over bravado.

I have found that while direct confidence quickly attracts the attention of others, a more subtle confidence can be equally if not more impactful. If you are as good as you think you are, others will take notice and speak well of you on your behalf. Just think about it for a minute as you examine the types of behaviors toward which you may have some affinity. Does arrogance energize you? Do self-centered people inspire you? I doubt you would say much in the affirmative to either question. The truth is, almost everyone I've dealt with throughout my life would rather be associated with, work with, or work for individuals who exude quiet senses of confidence rather than people who are self-absorbed. Having enough self-respect and being able to demonstrate a genuine respect for others will pay huge dividends in your personal and professional development efforts.

Never confuse humility with weakness. Those who continually demonstrate genuine humility as they deal with others get their attention. They can influence many on a much larger scale, attract better talent along the way, create additional confidence, and gain the respect and loyalty of those around them. If you subscribe to my belief that every business is a people business, how can this be anything but inspiring?

Visibility

The title of this chapter is very similar to other phrases used to describe how individuals are viewed and how the actions of others are influenced accordingly. All of us, regardless of where we are and what we represent, have some level of influence over others based on our actions. Certainly, the more visible we are to the masses, the larger our circle of influence becomes, and our shadow looms large over more people, resulting in an even greater impression.

Visibility is the act of being purposely noticed with the intent to both connect, and as a result, inspire others. This is not to be confused with what some have called management by walking around, simply an act on some managers parts to be seen and have others simply notice their presence. This is, in most cases, accompanied with little desire for interaction leaving limited ability to send or receive messages of import and inspiration. In fact, simply walking around in many cases creates a sense of insincerity and leaves an impression that it was just for show. You can quickly imagine this behavior has the potential to cause more harm than benefit. What I am talking about here is for you to take every reasonable opportunity to consistently reiterate the most important messages pertaining to the organization and facilitate opportunities to have real and meaningful conversations with the people within the organization to answer their questions, respond to their concerns, and offer clarity and reassurance. You need to do all you can to ensure they see and feel your presence is sincere. Each interaction offers an opportunity to actually be with them, become a part of what's on their minds, and to create a feeling of oneness. This type of interaction with your team will truly serve as an inspiration to them as well as yourself.

Visibility, when things are going well, is effective of course. Celebrating the successes of any organizations accomplishments builds that sense of togetherness and collective confidence. The real challenge is for leaders to resist the temptation to hide out or become far less visible during the challenging times. You must look at this as the most important time to be even more visible, not less. For all the reasons we talked about earlier, when people are unsure, stressed, have a fear of the unknown and are concerned about their future and the health of the business, that's the time for you to truly be there for them, unconditionally. Be bold and brave as a leader at any level and in any circumstance. I ask that you make a real investment in time, passion, energy, and thought, and don't cower at the real possibility you will become a part of the peoples vulnerabilities. Only inspiration will result!

Your objective should be to create an image of yourself not only that you are proud of but that can influence others to pass it on. I am not advocating forcing a specific style or approach on anyone. What I mean is that people look to others, particularly to those who can have influence over others' progression, for insights into what is expected and what is important. This offers those individuals direct perspectives on what they need to do not only to advance, but to fit within an organization.

I am hopeful that many of the behaviors I have discussed here are not new to you. I am equally hopeful and confident that what I have said here will resonate with you, and you will do all you can to remain cognizant of its importance and impact as you continue with your development journey. You will be far better for it as a result. Trust me!

> *Your greatest influence can happen while never saying a word.*

CHAPTER 9

THE BALANCING ACT: WORK AND LIFE

W e cannot have a discussion of personal and professional development without addressing what has become a topic of continuous debate: the balance of work and life. As conversations shift to people placing higher degrees of importance on the quality of their lives outside the workplace, leading or playing a role in a multigenerational workforce becomes an even greater challenge. Differing expectations among leaders, team members, and peers complicate the team building dynamic.

Many variables come into play here and determine for each of us how much of an issue achieving that right level of balance really is. I look at this as a personal issue or challenge and not one I can deal with simply by following the advice of the so-called experts. Staying with our prevailing theme, it all starts with you. It's about what works for your situation and helps you achieve that sense of having fun, making a difference, and learning each and every day. Disharmony outside the workplace can clearly have a significant impact on your ability to be at your best on the job or in the classroom. Your career aspirations should play a huge role as you make personal choices in your life. How you spend your free time, where you reside, your choice of partner, your cultural beliefs, and much more all play roles here.

For me it was a difficult yet clear decision. I knew I was going to be driven by my career, and work would consume my time and take priority as I encountered and made other choices in my life. That was really quite important at the onset of my professional development, and my behavior, reflected in the choices

It all starts with you.

I made along the way, underscored that importance.

I continually fought to achieve a blend of living a responsible and satisfying personal life while remaining committed to and focused on my responsibilities at work. Of course conflicts arose occasionally, and I had to make choices that were appropriate at those specific points in time. So it's important to remember it's the overall balance you are striving to achieve. At the same time, you must fully recognize there will always be a time when you will need to make choices that will throw that balance out of whack. Always make an attempt to make the right choices at the right time while being responsible and doing the right thing—without exception.

Throughout my career I have been continually faced with choosing between my work and my personal life. I would have to say, in the aggregate, work took top priority in a majority of cases, but my personal life rarely suffered. I made choices while considering all the circumstances involved, and in most cases the outcomes were positive. It is a significant help when others in your life—such as family, friends, and your peer group—truly recognize who you are, what you stand for, and what makes you happy.

Do not confuse this with being selfish. The choices we make early in our lives should take into account not only what works for us individually but also what's important to the people we choose to have close to us. You see, it's not just about your personal balance; it's about harmony in all aspects of your personal and professional worlds. When you do not take into account the considerations of others, selfishness can, and likely will, rear its ugly head.

The professionals I mentor tell me all the time how much they want to succeed, get ahead, take on additional responsibilities, and reach their full potential. Many have little to no idea what they are saying, and a far lower number have even a basic level of understanding. You see, when you place additional emphasis on your development, and you have your sights set on achieving much bigger and better things in your professional life, there is a price to pay that will impact your balance of work and life. Yes, we can apply all the advice and guidance discussed herein and even supplement those with the recommendations of others who perhaps see it differently. However, in almost every case, increased responsibility and span of control have an effect on the balance of work and life. It comes with the territory.

This does *not*, however, take away nor minimize the notion that we all can take actions to improve our personal situations. But in reality you may never reach the point at which you are consistently content with your balance in life. I feel you should think about that as you plan ahead for your professional development. In the end it's all about you and making choices that are best for your specific situation. Bringing a heightened sense of awareness to the dynamic is my primary objective here.

Having been faced with so many decisions in the balancing of work and life, I have always tried to make the right choices, or at least what I thought were the right choices at the time.

I fell short once in a while, but in most cases the choices I made worked out.

One in particular that comes to mind says it all. Recall how I spoke earlier of the unselfish nature of my supervisors when they chose to support my nomination to the corporate-sponsored, high-potential development program. What I didn't tell you was that it was a two-year assignment, with more than half of it spent at international and domestic locations far away from our Midwest headquarters. It was part of the assignment I referred to earlier during which I was heavily involved in a proposal process that kept me away from home for almost eight months straight. To add fuel to the fire, I learned on a Thursday evening that my first rotation would start on Friday at a location a thousand miles away. That same day my wife and I found out we were going to have another child; we already had a three-year-old son. I had to talk it over with my family and give my supervisors my decision to proceed or not that evening, as I would have to be on-site to start the assignment later the next day.

The dialogue at home was the easy part. My wife gave me her full support, so off I went. The continued challenge was that I saw my family only one time in those eight months—for a total of a two-day weekend in which I was present only about 50 percent of the time. I returned home just days before the birth of my daughter.

The hours I spent at work and the stress levels, while high, were very instructional. The assignment exposed me to a tremendous number of diverse experiences. Was it instrumental in my development? No question. Did my balance of work and life suffer? Yes, without a doubt. Is this for you? I have no idea.

Only you, considering your set of circumstances, can make this type of decision. There is no right or wrong here. You may take issue with my choices, and I can accept that, but that is not my point. It is up to you and those in your circle of influence to discuss the situation, assess the pros and cons, and in the end, do what you all feel is the right thing.

The story above highlights many points I made earlier. The decisions we make impact others, and that must be a primary consideration. Nothing significant comes without sacrifice. My energy, passion, and drive to make a difference in everything I did came into play. This continues to serve me well to this day. Finally, we should recognize that special opportunities like this won't come about very often, and if or when they do, we must be ready to openly consider all the variables and do what is best for all in the particular situation.

I thought I would offer the counterargument to my premise that working toward achieving a balance between work and life is an important aspect of your professional development. Yes, you read that correctly: there is a school of thought that goes so far as to say the entire concept of such a balance is highly over-

Forces other than you affect your balance of work and life.

rated. The many subscribers to this theory see trying to achieve some level of balance in our lives as piling on the guilt. They see the concept of work-life balance as something unnecessary to worry about. Some equate it to searching and striving for something that will always be elusive and, in doing so, impacting our ability to live our lives with higher degrees of spontaneity.

As best I can gather from all I have experienced on this subject, the basis for this notion is a more philosophical approach to how best to find your balance. The foundation for this argument is based upon setting your personal priorities, understanding what drives you, never compromising your personal values, and learning to roll with it a lot more. In essence, stop getting anxious over pursuing something that doesn't really exist.

I think there is some degree of merit in this approach because it's difficult to argue with the foundational behaviors mentioned above. However, that being said, and putting practical experiences in front of philosophy, I stand behind my views.

Throughout my adult life, I have posed the question of how to balance work and life quite often to those in my circle of influence, and I have received a tremendous amount of insight, advice, and suggestions along the way. Some of the feedback did not apply, or I determined it would not work for me. In other cases I found myself able to complement my skill set development with additional skills and behaviors. That seemed to have a positive effect on my ability to achieve a level of balance that was acceptable to me for my circumstances and the specific situation at the time.

Over the years I have kept a list of things I find helpful, and I have shared it with the countless number of people who have asked me about the work-life balance. As I achieved increasingly greater levels of success at work, people became more inquisitive about how I managed to treat everything in my life with the importance and priority it deserved. I wanted to be at my best if not each and every day, at least for an overwhelming majority of the time. Those inquiries told me countless numbers of others were struggling with the same issues I had dealt with throughout my entire career (and still do to a certain extent today).

Let me now share with you several of the concepts that have helped me. I am hopeful you will be able to relate to these in your own way and perhaps apply them to an appropriate extent.

Staying Positive

The first point I would like to emphasize here is the need to focus on staying positive. This in itself will *not* be the answer to any specific question, but having a positive approach and demeanor establishes a foundation on which to build all the rest of your actions. When your outlook remains positive, and you have a "can-do" approach, the influence you have on everyone around you will be noticeable, and these people will respond in kind. If you are not happy and have a difficult time staying positive, get to the root causes of your unhappiness and deal with them first and foremost.

I must admit, negativity and destructive criticism are truly pet peeves of mine. They are immediate turnoffs and directly impact my ability to stay focused and engaged. They are simply traits I have no time for, and although I've tried to be more understanding about them, I doubt I will be asked to teach sensitivity training on these topics anytime soon.

There is no way for you to achieve any sort of balance between work and life if you are unhappy and have a difficult time staying positive.

So what can you do to try to achieve a more optimistic perspective in your life? There are many thoughts here for you to consider. Try focusing on what you are blessed with and not what you may be lacking. Many people are far worse off than you—of that you can be sure. Be confident and comfortable with the choices you make; embrace and share the positive outcomes and learn from the less-than-positive outcomes. Try hard to view every obstacle as a challenge, not as an issue or problem, and use them as opportunities to energize yourself to excel, overcome, and move ahead. Just the way I did on the mountain that day!

Focus on waking up with a positive perspective every day. Try to set a positive tone right upfront to the best of your ability. Do all you can to surround yourself with people who have positive outlooks. I am not asking you to abandon your relationships with people who struggle with positivity, but I am asking you to accept the fact that we often reflect the environments in which we operate. Work hard to surround yourself with positivity.

The next thing I want you to remember is not to forget who you are and what makes you tick. You have a personality that is yours and yours alone. Once you combine it with your skill sets and life experiences, it makes you even more unique. Reminding yourself of this is important and directly applies to what you set out to accomplish in your professional life. That being the case, the goals you have established are compatible and directly in line with your personality and professional makeup. This simply serves as a real indicator of whether you are able to follow through on what you set out to do. There are many ways to the endgame, and I can assure you, no two paths are identical in direction or pace. A realignment of your objectives and goals may be in order here, and it may serve as the new start for which you are searching.

If you must whine, embrace the art of talking to yourself.

Prioritize

In staying with the theme of potentially realigning your goals and objectives, an obvious yet difficult concept to master consistently is the ability to prioritize. But I am suggesting you take it on with a vengeance. Have the ability to know what's in front of you, perform triage, and get on to those things with the greatest degree of importance as you've defined it. How will you spend your time? What kinds of tasks or issues comprise what you put on your calendar? Is it time to look at additional delegations of tasks? Do you really need to be involved in everything you actually spend your time on?

Perhaps delegating tasks to others will have a dual purpose. On the one hand, delegation will buy you some additional time; on the other hand, if done properly, it will serve as a developmental exercise for others. I have continually delegated responsibility since the early years of my leadership development. It always seems to work very well for me and for the members of my team.

How about examining the value of the specific task? Looking at the amount of value added—if there is any at all—to the things you choose to spend your time on can be a tremendously valuable experience. Proponents of "lean"—the art of eliminating waste—have done many studies that suggest anywhere from 10 percent to 90 percent of the tasks we spend time on are of little to no value. Successful individuals and organizations focus their time and attention on things that add value and ignore, pass over, or remove the non-value-added tasks as part of a large-scale lean implementation.

I will offer a few suggestions for determining whether a task has value and can truly offer a direct form of competitive differentiation for you and/or your organization. You should also ask yourself this question: As a consumer, if you had a limited budget and were looking for a specific product, would you be willing to pay for any of the waste that may exist in the product manufacturer's design and/or processes? What if this means you'd pay a higher price than you would for the same product from a more lean, cost-effective supplier? The answer is most likely an obvious no. So why don't you work to design out or simply eliminate those things you spend your time on that add no value? If you do not directly control them, determine who the process owner is, explain how you might work together to eliminate the waste, and create value through a reduction in throughput time. Once you become comfortable with differentiating the efforts that do and do not offer value, you can begin the process of filling up your calendar with tasks that only add value.

I understand this is far easier said than done, particularly in large organizations where processes are high in number and complexity. Look at it as both a challenge and an opportunity to become involved in improving not only your own time management but also your organization's efficiency. Frankly, I wouldn't even consider working for an organization in which delivering value to the customer is not a top priority. But if that's the case, given what I see going on in all forms of global competition, many organizations will fail and eventually disappear. The answer here, contrary to what some may tell you, is *not* to negotiate more lead time but always to find a way to do more in less time.

What else can I suggest to help you become more comfortable with setting priorities? First, remember what I have talked about regarding doing what you have said you will do, or, if you don't do what you said you would, making it right in the end. Clearly understanding your commitments and establishing time frames and deadlines in which to accomplish them will help you establish priorities. While I have never been one to spend a lot of time on the negative, there is something to be said about weighing the consequences of falling short on all that is in front of you.

> *Work smarter not harder.*

Perhaps this will help you as it has helped me place a better emphasis on the tasks at hand, and thus reduce the negative aftermath as much as possible. Cleaning up a mess after the fact is not a valuable way to spend your time if doing so could have been avoided in the first place. I have also found interweaving some things I enjoy personally while focusing on professional matters recharges my energy levels and adds staying power when I might otherwise back away. This in turn allows me to become more efficient, and, in the end, to accomplish more in a shorter amount of time.

Saying No

One of the hardest things I had to learn was how and when to say no. It's not as easy as it first sounds. Saying no requires courage. This is particularly true if you are an individual with a positive, can-do working spirit. When others see you that way, they don't naturally expect to hear you say no.

Not everything can hold top priority.

The concept of saying no may seem foreign and in some circumstances distasteful. But if you are to make time during your day for what's truly important and adds value, this is not negotiable; it is a must do. As in all things, there are both constructive and destructive ways to say no. It must be accompanied by a degree of reasoning that comes after mindful consideration. Or, if time does not allow that, a quick, on-your-feet set of reasons can be effective.

Base your decision either to say no or accept a task on several factors. Sometimes you don't have a choice due to politics, organizational hierarchy, or other variables; in that case, grin and bear it, and do the best you can—then move on. Save the fight for what's right for another day. I have *always* found it extremely helpful to remind myself that each and every time I said no to something that was wasteful and brought no value, I was at the same time making room to tackle issues that added value and had a higher degree of importance. That is what this entire discussion is about.

At one time I had a propensity to fill my calendar from 5:30 a.m. until 7:00 or 8:00 p.m. every day. That was directly related to the problems I had with never saying no. I had an open-door policy that many of my team members utilized, and I wanted to be a highly visible and approachable representative of the supervisory ranks. That made saying no a significant challenge for me. For whatever reason, having a workday that was full kept me busy and perhaps gave me an inflated sense of self-importance. It took a swift kick in my backside from the world's best executive assistant to snap me out of that terribly inefficient set of practices.

While you may not be fortunate enough at this point to have this capability, you must rely on yourself and those around you to help you make these types of choices. My assistant was the instigator of my call to action. In the absence of someone like that, you must take this on yourself if you are to make any headway. I was constantly running behind and had little to no time in between obligations, and the level of dysfunction and frustration I levied on others as a result needed to stop. My assistant taught me to think through the commitments I was planning to make, which allowed me the opportunity to see the value, degree of importance, and priority through another set of eyes. I learned to translate that to scheduling efficiency. Whether it's an assistant, peers, or mentors who may be proficient in managing their days, seek the insights of others. Over time, with patience and reinforcement, you will find that right balance when filling your calendar.

What did I do to deal with the constantly growing demands on my time? I had to understand and accept that sometimes I did it to myself. I was driven to be involved and to remain engaged. No one has truly ever forced me to participate in something; I always gave my consent. Do you bring this on yourself, or would you falsely consider yourself the constant victim?

You must accept that you play a huge role in deciding how to spend your time. I have always had difficulty accepting the fact that I can't do it all; I can't play a large role in everything. I used to view that as giving in, lying down, or accepting mediocrity. In reality that is not the case. I have found that recognizing I can't do it all and coming to grips with thinking otherwise was quite helpful in developing my ability to say no. I also have tried to place more emphasis on the things I really want to do, balancing them with what needs to be done. This is not always as easy as it sounds, but again, raising an awareness of energy and need has helped me do a better job of deciding how best to allocate my time.

In the end, as always, what you spend your time on is up to you. Remember in doing that, to always organize your thoughts to enable you to assess their values, degrees of importance, and priorities. At the same time, it pays to know there are just some things that are out of your control, so accept that fact and move on.

Saying no can be a very powerful action.

Risk Management

The next thing I would like you to think about is trying to look ahead daily with an emphasis on averting a crisis—or, as others call it, practicing risk management. I have learned quite a bit about leading through crisis during my tenure as a senior leader. But I have also learned how to be better at looking ahead, trying to improve my ability to anticipate crises or conflicts, and developing plans to address and minimize risk.

I cannot accurately quantify how much time I have wasted on wallowing in the details of crisis recovery. In so many cases, I could have avoided the issue had I taken the time to think about, anticipate, and plan for it in advance. This advice applies across the complete spectrum of possible crises, from the overscheduling of meetings right on up to applying risk management processes on projects of a larger scale. While I tend to agree that mastering this proactive behavior is easier for some than for others, learning to anticipate better and planning ahead on a more consistent basis will pay huge dividends on improving your balance of work and life.

One of the best pieces of advice I can give you is to do all you can, call on all your experiences, and use your network to discuss things that could negatively impact progress. Try to leave no stone unturned; anything goes here. The point is, you can't prevent something from impacting you if you don't know about it even being a possibility in advance. You should work smartly to identify and analyze the risks and quantify what their impact would be if they came to fruition. Try to assess the impact by again drawing on all your experiences and those of others. There are solutions to every challenge, so it follows that developing a solution to eliminate, reduce, or absorb any aftermath of the risk is the next area of focus. Once you choose a solution, keeping a close eye on the progress of your plan is vital.

You have only so many hours in a day to allocate. You have to take care of your physical needs, you have professional obligations, and the social aspects of your life offer the balance. My thought here is simple: since your time is truly limited, do all you can not to spend any of it dealing with issues you could have avoided in the first place.

Risk management—that is, avoiding, averting, or eliminating the potential to have to deal with crisis management—will go a long way toward allowing you to spend more time on the things that truly add value. It takes time and effort, that's true. But you will find that acting in a proactive manner simply makes sense, and, in the end, will take less time than dealing with any crisis aftermath.

As hard as we try, finding the right level of balance in work and life and doing a better job of how we manage our time is an art. It's easier for some than for others. It's personal, and it's all about what works for us individually and collaboratively. Try to keep to a minimum the level of anxiety focusing on this creates, and do the very best you can, recognizing that nothing will ever be perfect. Always bring your best to whatever situation your work or family focus offers and stay in the present at every opportunity. Do what it takes to learn, have fun, and make a difference each and every day.

Isn't this what we all want for ourselves?

CHAPTER 10

THE BALL'S IN YOUR COURT

I want to thank you so very much for taking the time to allow me the privilege of sharing my development perspectives with you. Writing a book was not my dream, but discussing my experiences with you in the hope that I could make a difference in your life became a passion of mine over time. It fits right in with the themes I have repeated in this volume multiple times: learn, have fun, and make a difference each and every day, and do not accept mediocrity as an option. I thank you for letting me help you to become the very best you can be.

In the previous nine chapters, we have shared a lot. From the very beginning, I stated emphatically that taking responsibility for your professional development is nonnegotiable if you want to increase the probability of reaching your full potential. I was also clear that when you accept this responsibility seriously, a tremendous time commitment follows. Unless you're one of the few lucky ones, driving your self-development is intensive and demands your time, patience, persistence, and flexibility. I would much rather do all I can do to be the best I can be—with no regrets.

We have explored the importance of examining yourself relative to your skills, behaviors, and values and spent a lot of quality time thinking about what you want your legacy to be. I encouraged you to seek out the perspectives of others who can help you better understand what it takes to achieve the goals in your short-term and long-term views. We took quite a bit of time to discuss the meaning and value of mentoring, and I provided a significant amount of guidance on how to choose a mentor. Along with taking responsibility for your professional development, the value and contribution of a strong mentor-mentee relationship cannot be overstated. We also discussed the art of listening, particularly to feedback from others that may not be what you want to hear, and its degree of importance.

I wouldn't count on being lucky.

Creating an inventory of your skills and identifying your shortcomings was a huge step. We explored defining how you might go about developing the skills that are required for your progression.

We transitioned into the more visual and administrative portion of our journey by describing a simple career development timeline concept you could duplicate and use with your own data. Visualizing where you have been and where you plan to go can be a motivator to push you forward. It also serves as a constant reminder of your current view of the end objective and offers you the opportunity to rethink that at any time.

I want to be clear about what I am really looking for you to do here. You may find career planning tools online that are more to your liking than those I've offered herein. If that is the case, I certainly encourage you to seek them out and apply them to your situation. The primary purpose of our discussion throughout this book has not necessarily been the tools with which to document your professional journey but putting you in a position to create all the waypoints. Regardless of the tool you use, know that each and every concept we've discussed applies to you, without exception. Yet without your full commitment and engagement, no tool or process will suffice.

Our discussion then took a different course as it was my desire to introduce to you—and emphasize the importance of understanding, developing, and applying—the soft skills. As I look back over my career, I can truly say the role these played in my development and professional success was immeasurable. There is not much you can do in life alone, and these skills are instrumental in developing passionate, energetic, committed, and high-performance work teams at all levels.

Immediately following our discussion of the soft skills was an examination of behaviors and how we carry ourselves throughout the day. Remember that the shadow of leadership you cast is vital to how others will see you and what conclusions, right or wrong, they will draw from their observations. Your leadership shadow will either enable or impede your personal development and the development of your team.

We then focused our attention on balancing our personal and professional lives. Keeping in mind that one size does not fit all, we discussed ways to determine what level of balance works for you and those around you. We explored both sides of the argument in terms of how important achieving some level of balance is to each of us. I always find it challenging to separate the different aspects of my life completely, and I usually find that any pleasure or disarray in one part of my life impacts the other parts. The magic is how we deal with all of this.

Now that we've done all the preparation for creating your personal way forward, what's next?

The three major thoughts I want to leave you with as we complete our first journey together center around the power of a network, the art of giving back, and a call to action.

The Power of a Network

Imagine for a moment that you are at a point in your life where you can tell you need a change in your situation. It doesn't matter if you are still a student, in an entry-level role within some organization, or have the benefit of more experience; your current status does not change the way you should go about planning. You have a solid understanding of your education levels and the skill sets you possess. You also have the benefit of all of the experiences that have been part of your life journey thus far.

In this book I have strongly encouraged you to spend some time thinking about the long-term and your professional and personal aspirations. But you realize you can't go from where you currently are to where you want to be in the long-term at this point in time. This obviously requires gaining access to different experiences and skill sets you do not yet possess but can with time and the right guidance. Or perhaps you or someone you know needs some guidance not necessarily related to career or development planning. I have found building and maintaining a wide, deep, and powerful network, far beyond the mentor process, can be one of the most impactful things you can do. Another way to look at it is that all those who mentor you are in your network, yet all those in your network may not serve the role of mentoring you. Over the years, when I have needed guidance or advice, I've simply tapped in to the personal and professional network I built over time with individuals I knew or felt strongly would help steer me or someone else in the right direction.

Let me share a story with you that occurred quite recently that will add some clarity to what we are talking about here. I was in a meeting with some entrepreneurs, exploring an investment opportunity related to a medical device. The topic of cancer came up as a matter of course within the discussion. I spoke about a fellow board member who had just been diagnosed with an aggressive form of brain cancer for which treatment options were limited and experimental. Coincidentally, one of the entrepreneurs mentioned that an associate of his, a person in his network, is the world's most recognized authority on the diagnosis and treatment of that exact disease. After some discussion, he went on to contact the individual regarding my friend's health challenges. After I made a quick call to ensure my friend and his family would support making a direct connection with the physician, the rest of the dialogue took place directly between the patient and the specialist. My network, in that case consisting of the entrepreneurs and their network, was instrumental in making that connection a reality! Things like that don't simply occur; they happen as a direct result of having a network.

You will need to make a commitment to and focus on building a network. Each and every individual you meet potentially has something to offer: a unique perspective or capability, or access to some of the same within his or her network. This does not occur overnight; it takes time. The sooner you make a concerted effort to build a powerful network, the sooner it will develop and the more robust and effective it will become over time.

While the mentor development process we talked about earlier is similar in nature, there are distinct differences. The mentor relationship can be a bit more focused and formal and relates more specifically to personal development. Your network will likely be more diverse in composition; some people in it may serve as mentors, but the relationships will likely be more ad hoc. Like those in your mentor group, these individuals can come from both your personal and professional lives. You simply need to make building your network a priority and do what it takes to make it happen. I can think of a countless number of examples in which a network was instrumental in assisting me and others along the way, and the connection brought on action and results.

The world is filled with talented, energetic people who are more than happy to lend a helping hand and give back in their own ways. It may not be that easy for you, but nothing worthwhile ever comes without effort. I can't encourage you enough to get energized about filling your network with individuals who you and others feel can expose you to the skills, behaviors, experiences, and capabilities you need in order to move forward. In many instances, and in all walks of life, those individuals who are truly making differences stand out; they are the ones about whom others talk. Your ability to gain access to them will not happen on its own. Again, you need to get ouside your comfort zone, build a more robust network filled with those who can make real differences in your life, and make the absolute most of each and every relationship.

> *Networks can expand your solution set to help you solve problems.*

True relationships don't just happen. Individuals can meet unexpectedly, a connection can form, and a true relationship can result over time. But even in those instances, the development and maturity of the relationship takes a tremendous amount of work. It follows that you should better understand what the relationship building process takes and why it is important before I spend any more time impressing upon you the important place these relationships should hold in your development and success.

You may recall I mentioned my fear of direct sales early on in this book. I simply had no time for picking up the phone or being in a situation where I wanted or needed something from someone I did not know. I would avoid putting myself in those positions whenever possible. I put that shortcoming on my career development plan early on, in one of the very first versions of my road map. I was working in a product and service business where relationships in all aspects of the value chain were critical, so I had no choice: I needed to face my fears and deal with them. So what did I do?

I had a few things going for me. I am social by nature, and, as you may have gathered, I am quite outgoing and energetic in everything I attempt to accomplish. The primary issue I had was feeling comfortable with asking someone for something I needed. It became more complex and difficult when I did not know the person or organization. To make it even more difficult, I am quite confident and surefooted, so my natural tendency was always to try to go at it alone and get it done in my own way, with no help from others.

In discussions with my supervisors and my mentors, we examined the possibility of my leading a marketing and sales organization for our government business. It would serve as a means to get me the exposure I required to understand better the need for and value of building relationships. It required me to get far more exposure to the customer side of our business. The potential role seemed like a perfect developmental opportunity for me; customer relationship management is instrumental to the success of any business, so its applicability was evident.

After those initial discussions, all the issues I've talked about raised their ugly heads: getting out of my comfort zone, the fear of failure, my lack of affinity for the sales domain, my concern over the unknown, and being held accountable for the orders and sales performance of our company. But, as I have tried to impress upon you, more times than not, nothing great comes easily. I started to reflect on all the positives that could come out of taking on such an opportunity, and, just as I've suggested in this book, I found myself getting more energized, excited, and impatient as I waited for the opportunity to come to fruition.

The opportunity presented itself in due time, and I jumped in right away. I built a team of professionals who had tremendous levels of expertise in all aspects of the sales and marketing value chain. In working together over a three-year period, we built a very successful organization that not only delivered on its commitments but demonstrated very clearly to me the power and importance of relationships. I spent a majority of my time outside the comforts of the corporate office and immersed myself in our customers' domains. Slowly I began to understand the importance of relationships in our ability to differentiate ourselves in the eyes of our customers from others that served the same markets.

That realization was instrumental in my converting all my misgivings about the importance and contribution that building relationships played in our company's success to a real skill strength I was then able to pass on to those I mentored, counseled, and coached. And, as all that was going on, I learned I could deal better with my fear of cold calling by always remembering the power and utility of building relationships. It became a skill I focused on continuously throughout the remainder of my professional life and continues to serve me quite well to this day.

Now, what does that mean for you? What can you take away from my experience? While it demonstrates yet another example of the utility of having a development plan and focusing on skill refinement, and the value and contribution of a mentor, there is so much more to it. Because of how strongly I feel about the important role building true relationships will play in both your personal and professional lives, I want to give you some insight on some of the more important things to take into consideration as you grow, develop, and spend more time and energy on strengthening your relationship building capabilities.

Throughout my professional career I built some very powerful teams, developed and implemented business strategies that had great impact, and served in positions that resulted in tremendous growth for our business. I also realized that relationships were the foundations for all that success. Regardless of whether the relationships were with peers, mentors, team members, or customers, I tried hard to think about what the common characteristics were that made them truly prolific. Those relationships were far different from the much more common, casual acquantainces we all have in our lives.

First and foremost, people are drawn to others who speak with integrity and are truthful in not only everything they say but in all they do. This is true in all cultures. The importance of truth and integrity is further underscored when you are dealing with cultures that place great value on your word and doing what you say versus immediately bringing out the contract language to remind all concerned of their legal commitments. Dealing with many Asian cultures throughout my professional life has taught me the importance of one's word and how critical it is to do as you say you will do.

Second, I learned through all my experiences that treating everyone with the degree of respect he or she deserves is vital. While the chain of command is always a consideration, all people—regardless of who they are or what their titles are—deserve your respect. I thought of the lobby receptionist at the headquarters as one of our largest customers. While in some others' eyes she was merely a receptionist, to me she was the first face of the company's brand people saw when entering the lobby. Because she was deserved, I treated her as important and she helped me with information and access to people that made me much more effective in my role. Again, many cultures place high degrees of importance on titles, ages, responsibilities, and education, but for me, I simply treat everyone I meet with all the respect I can deliver.

Third, while some live their lives trying to get more than their fair share, I have always found you will get what you deserve and possibly more by treating all those you deal with as fairly as possible. Customers want value for what they pay. Deliver it as promised, unconditionally. Look for solutions to situations in which all concerned come out feeling like they have won. No one likes to feel like he or she has ended up on the short end of anything. So work hard to compromise, be fair, and recognize the needs of the others involved.

There is a cultural impact to this issue as well. Many careers are destroyed when people lose face in the eyes of others. It's treated almost as a sin that's not soon forgotten, so it is important you understand this and keep it in mind when you are trying hard to be fair in your dealings with others.

Fourth, sincerity is another characteristic that comes to the forefront. While closely tied to honesty, sincerity has a lot to do with how you deliver a message and how people receive it. You can deliver the truth in a way that comes across as mistruth and vice versa, so sincerity and believability are important. The *best* way to be believable, and for your intentions to serve you well continuously, is always to do what you say. Sound familiar?

Fifth, flexibility and the ability to compromise will always serve you well as you work at building and strengthening the quality and number of your relationships. If you tend to put people in the mind-set that it's your way or it's over—well, trust me, *it's over*! Everyone likes to feel that his or her needs, contributions, beliefs, positions, and ideas have value and deserve consideration. You have already learned how important practicing active listening and diversity of thought are in improving your creativity. Practicing those traits, along with always trying to find a way to modify your position through compromise, will truly help you form good relationships that will continue to serve you well over time.

Finally, another one of my biggest pet peeves is when I hear from people only when they need something. This certainly puts the quality and nature of our relationships in question. Behaving in a more consistent and balanced fashion over the long haul will serve you well. I have always made it a point to make contact routinely with the many people I have had true relationships with over time and work very hard to keep up with them. With certain individuals it is easier, perhaps due to the fact that our dealings might be more current. Regardless, don't let the passing of time or the lack of a true need deter you from continuously working on maintaining your relationships. You will learn how important it truly is and how much impact it can have on your ability to get things done.

I have alluded several times to the challenges and opportunities you will face in trying to build international relationships. Each and every one of us is a product of our environment and upbringing. Despite that, we sometimes fall into the trap of believing that all others view and value things in a similar fashion. This could not be further from the truth. Those who have had any international experience will quickly tell those who have none about the tremendous challenges that cultural differences create when building relationships. Ultimately the degree of success one might achieve in doing business globally is directly related to this. While going into all those differences by regions of the world has a place in another book, suffice it to say, it is vitally important that you recognize this upfront; it will serve you very well to immerse yourself in learning all you can in advance of having to operate in any culturally diverse activity so you can best learn what to expect and how to deal with all that will come your way.

In closing out this discussion about relationships, I hope I have in some way convinced you of their degree of importance in all aspects of our lives and have offered some food for thought on what you can do to build more and better relationships. I am quite confident in saying the quantity and quality of relationships have been most instrumental factors in both my personal and professional successes.

> *The quality of the outcome will certainly be a result of your advance preparation.*

Given the vital nature of building and maintaining relationships, do not leave it to chance. Having taken relationship building from a critical skill shortage to a true character strength in my career, I can tell you it takes time, energy, and persistence. I have made this one of my biggest areas of focus when helping others as they strive to become all they can be.

Obviously the more relationships and contacts you develop, the greater and more diverse perspectives you will gain. Stay strong and remain focused, and in the end all of this will contribute in a significant way to your personal progress. This is a very important part of a long personal journey, but the rewards, successes, and even the challenges you'll meet along the way are what make all of it worthwhile. It's all part of what defines us.

Giving Back

Now let's turn our attention to the art of giving back. Perhaps the social networking, global media phenomenon has created a heightened awareness of what's going on both domestically and internationally. In turn, this has deepened our appreciation for how fortunate we are to have what we have; and that in part has encouraged a higher level of social responsibility. Regardless of the origin, I can tell you the opportunities to give back are boundless. There are many ways in which you can give back, and that aspect is a very personal choice that I will leave up to you. I will also stand behind my contention that by giving back, you're helping yourself in parallel, which is exactly why I included the topic in this book on career development. If you're still questioning its applicability, let me explain further because, as you will see, the art of giving back enables so many of the desirable outcomes we have addressed directly in this book.

The first point I will raise is that by giving back you are creating valuable content for your personal makeup and your résumé. You are building skills that may or may not align with your specific professional role, but they will add a diverse set of accomplishments to your experience base.

Next, in many cases giving back offers you a real opportunity to make a large impact, create value, and make a true difference in a shorter amount of time than you perhaps could otherwise. The world of volunteerism is overflowing with tons of desire, but many of these opportunities lack organization and leadership. What a chance for you to step in, take charge, and lead a team of individuals to accomplish something significant on behalf of others!

Remember that in some cases giving back is done on an individual basis. Even if that's the case, the recipient of your goodwill naturally becomes part of your network.

I serve as a member of the board of trustees for a small but highly regarded liberal arts college near my hometown. As part of my responsibilities as a trustee, I serve on a small scholarship committee. The role of this committee is to seek out five students annually (out of hundreds who apply) who set the standard of excellence in academic achievement and who possess what it takes to make real differences. The award for each is a full year of tuition, paid in full, from a large endowment established by a past graduate. While the applications come mostly from students who have truly excelled in their classroom efforts, there are those who have gone to the extreme in dedicating of their time and energy to the benefit of others. At the same time, they gain tremendous amounts of respect from their fellow students, faculty, staff, and college leaders at all levels along the way. Far more often than not, these are the students to whom we award the annual scholarship. This is a great example of giving back and paying it forward. It's truly powerful.

Throughout this book I have stressed the importance of learning, having fun, and making a difference each and every day. In regard to giving back, I cannot think of many other things in life that you can apply a portion of your discretionary time to that will provide such an immediate and continuous supply of opportunities for you to experience. It's up to you how much you want to take advantage of those opportunities and how important giving back will be in your life. I ask you to do your homework and choose wisely from the unlimited opportunities afforded you; don't be discouraged if, after making a choice, it doesn't turn out the way you hoped. Look at each as a platform from which to excel.

Finally, let's talk about your giving back in a different way. To set the stage, I am hopeful those of you reading this book run the spectrum in terms of where you might be in your development process. I am sure a great many of you are in the early, formative years of your careers while others represent the more experienced and established population of professionals who are looking to jump-start their careers. Regardless of where you find yourself on that continuum, you can reflect on your current and past states as you were or are working hard to establish a network of mentors. Whether you are a mentor, a mentee, or perhaps both, or whether you are simply part of a network, you always have something to offer another person. I have heard students in the classes I have taught and those with minimal professional experience express concern over their perceived lack of anything to offer anyone. This couldn't be further from reality, and I tell them that very directly and firmly. A bit of sound advice: sharing a skill or simply lending an ear is something we can all offer. When someone needs our time, we have not only the opportunity but also the obligation to give back in some way, shape, or form. Yes, each of us—including *you*! No exceptions.

You see, that is what I am going to ask of you as we end this phase of our professional journey together: while you begin the process of taking responsibility for your development, look out for others who could benefit from an affiliation with you.

Be proactive, reach out when you sense the need, and respond through action whether you are called upon or not.

While you become more focused on your development, do all you can to help others learn, have fun, and make differences each and every day of their lives.

A Call to Action

Let me close with something I say often and to so many as I speak publicly about my experiences. I'm not really sure when it happened, but sometime early in my career I thought I wanted to play a role in making something special happen. As time passed, I transitioned from thinking that was what I wanted to *knowing* that was what I *needed* to do. I became driven in every way to do all I could to make that a reality.

At the end of my last role in a company I had worked for my entire career, all my efforts and my team's efforts resulted in outcomes that were undeniably very special. As I have already mentioned, we had been faced with tremendous challenges, such as competition, global dynamics, and turmoil in the economy and in specific marketplaces we served, and that was just the start. These challenges and their impacts were underscored by disease that impacted air travel, the 9/11 terrorist attacks, and crude oil prices. If all that weren't enough, internally we were faced with cost challenges and employee morale issues at a time when we were implementing the principles of lean in every aspect of our company's value chain.

The challenges were substantial, and at the time they seemed almost insurmountable. There was a point very early on in that assignment when I felt somewhat overwhelmed and even disinterested. I think I missed the comforts of the business I had just left, which was running very well. You see, even at that point in my career, I was comfortable, and I was unknowingly accepting mediocrity. My supervisors did not see mediocrity as an option for me; the board saw a challenge and felt I was the right person to take it on. Those people saw in me what I, in a way, doubted in myself. But as we built our team, developed our strategies, and began the difficult journey toward recovery and growth, the progress came steadily, momentum built, and the results spoke for themselves. What had started out for me as an assignment

I really didn't want, turned out to be what I now say was the most exciting and rewarding chapter of my professional life. I was truly part of something special, and I know that now.

I wish the same for you. If you take ownership, put yourself in a position to make a difference, and make those opportunities become realities, you too can be part of something special.

What life offers us should not just be left to chance. My premise all along has been that what we get out of life all starts with accepting the responsibility to develop our path ahead, doing what it takes, and following through to drive results. I have encouraged you to accept this tremendous responsibility of making the most of your life for the relatively small amount of time we are on Earth. You will know, in your own way, when you have made progress in achieving the successes you set out to achieve. Life should be all about pleasure, but recognize that we must earn this pleasure.

I want to challenge you to make your life truly something special and achieve something that is unique and yours alone—an outstanding result because of what you were willing to put into its creation and not because you simply settled for what came your way. You can have a most powerful impact on what you can accomplish in your life, and if you are willing to do what it takes, you can turn what you wish for into reality.

Looking back on both my personal and professional journeys, I recognize and believe all the hard work, sacrifice, setbacks, and impediments were instrumental in laying the groundwork for my creating this tremendous life I am blessed with today. But even more than that, they set the stage well for me to continue to become even more and accomplish many other things in whatever time lies ahead.

I view my life as a gift, and I want you to see yours the same way. Life is a privilege, and we have the responsibility to take advantage of the opportunities it brings.

It's now up to you. Are you ready for the challenge? Actions speak much more loudly than words. The time to act is *now*! Never remain in a position in which mediocrity is present and tolerated. For me that was rarely an option, and I am hopeful the same will be true for you.

Mediocrity is not an option!

ABOUT THE AUTHOR

Robert M. Chiusano is a highly accomplished corporate executive and the current president of a consulting firm focused on executive coaching, career planning, leadership development, and operational excellence. Throughout his professional career, he has applied his high-energy, passion, and experience-based approach to mentor thousands of professionals with their career foci and has continued sharing his message through public speaking.

Robert is also an adjunct business professor at the University of Iowa and a lecturer whose message—mediocrity is not an option—has helped those he has mentored to plan their professional legacies. By combining passionate, serious, and humorous stories that you will not soon forget, Robert provides a take-charge approach to help people create plans for their careers and lives.

Robert is a graduate of Hudson Valley Community College, the State University of New York at Buffalo, and the University of Iowa. He holds a bachelor of science degree in engineering and a master's degree in business administration. Robert and his wife, Joanne, live in Springville, Iowa, and have two children, Robert and Christina.

Made in the USA
Monee, IL
26 February 2021

61419206R00125